FAMILY BIBLE STORY

JACOB

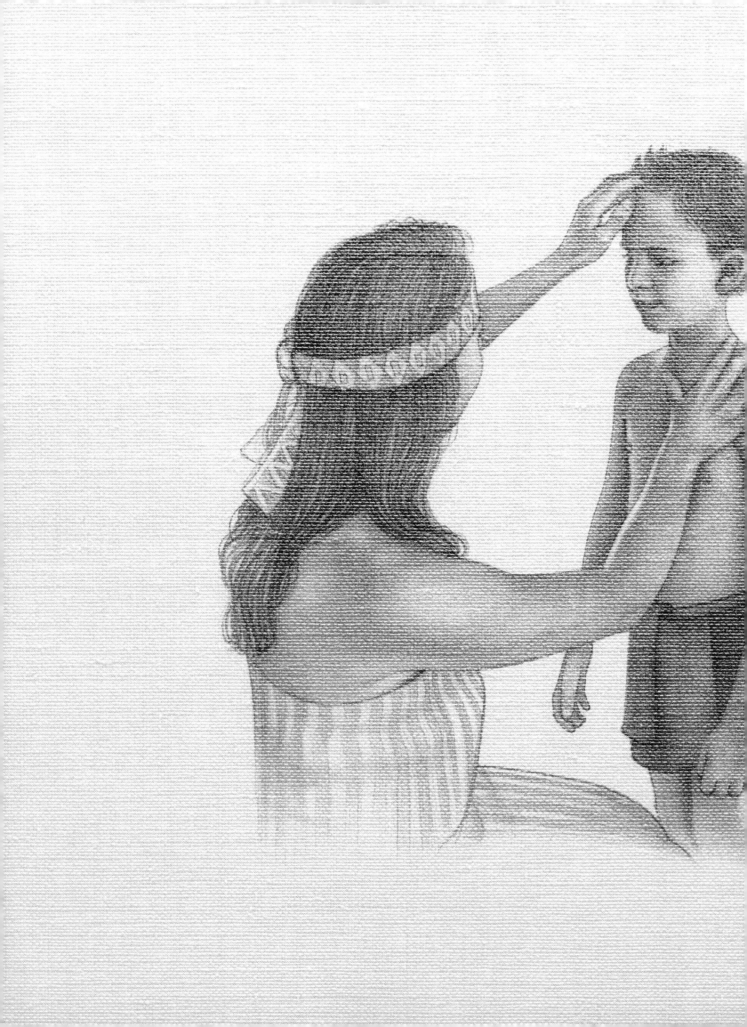

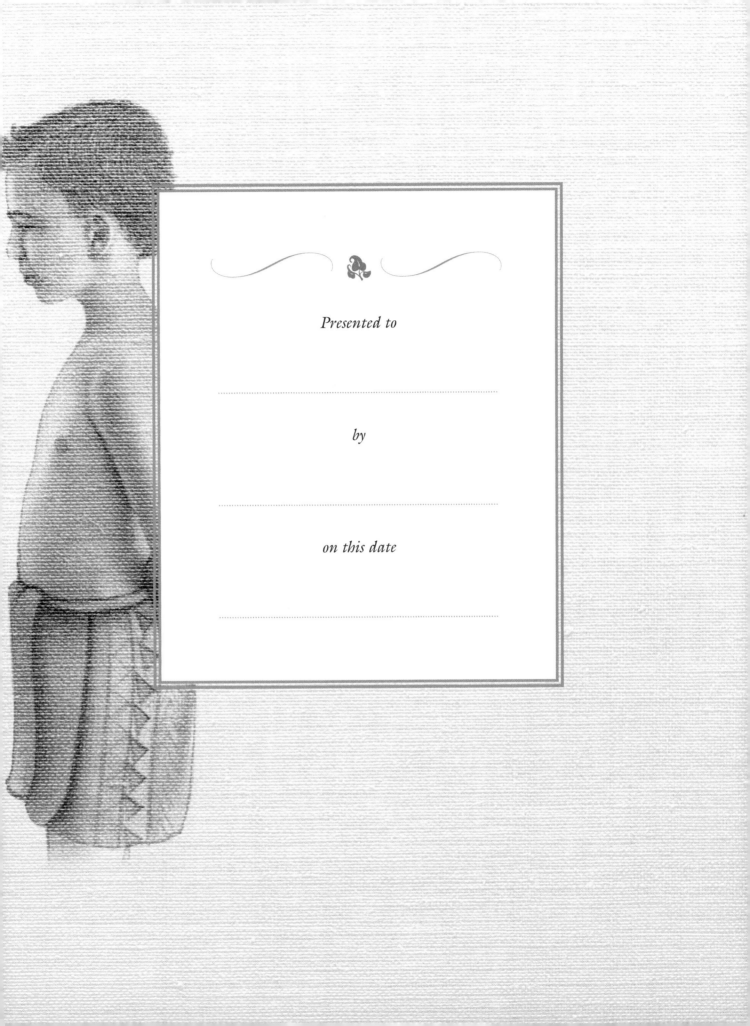

Presented to

....

by

....

on this date

....

To order, call

1-800-765-6955

or go to

www.familybiblestory.com

✦

For information on other Review and Herald® products

visit us at

www.reviewandherald.com

FAMILY BIBLE STORY

JACOB

Text by
RUTH REDDING BRAND

Color paintings by Joel Spector
Pencil illustrations by Darrel Tank

REVIEW AND HERALD® PUBLISHING ASSOCIATION
HAGERSTOWN, MD 21740

Pencil Illustrations copyright © 2004 by Darrel Tank. All rights reserved under the Pan-American and International Copyright conventions.

Scriptures credited to ICB are quoted from the *International Children's Bible, New Century Version,* copyright © 1983, 1986, 1988 by Word Publishing, Dallas, Texas 75039. Used by permission.

Bible texts credited to Jerusalem are from *The Jerusalem Bible,* copyright © 1966 by Darton, Longman & Todd, Ltd., and Doubleday & Company, Inc. Used by permission of the publisher.

Bible texts credited to New Jerusalem are from *The New Jerusalem Bible,* copyright © 1985 by Darton, Longman & Todd, Ltd., and Doubleday & Company, Inc. Used by permission of the publisher.

Bible texts credited to NRSV are from the New Revised Standard Version of the Bible, copyright © 1989 by the Division of Christian Education of the National Council of the Churches of Christ in the U.S.A. Used by permission.

Bible texts credited to RSV are from the Revised Standard Version of the Bible, copyright © 1946, 1952, 1971, by the Division of Christian Education of the National Council of the Churches of Christ in the U.S.A. Used by permission.

Bible texts credited to TEV are from the *Good News Bible*—Old Testament: Copyright © American Bible Society 1976, 1992; New Testament: Copyright © American Bible Society 1966, 1971, 1976, 1992.

This book was
Edited by Richard W. Coffen
Copyedited by Jocelyn Fay, Delma Miller, and James Cavil
Designed by Trent Truman
Cover art by Joel Spector
Typeset: Galliard 13/22

PRINTED IN U.S.A.

09 08 07 06 05   5 4 3 2 1

R&H Cataloging Service
Family Bible Story: Jacob
    V.

    1. Bible Stories. I. Brand, Ruth Redding

        220.9505

ISBN 0-8280-1852-9 hardcover
ISBN 0-8280-1853-7 paperback

DEDICATED TO

Gail Hunt—

artist, designer, musician,
dreamer, genius, and

the inspiration for this book.

CONTENTS

ABOUT THESE BOOKS

During the 1980s the Review and Herald administration authorized research for the Family Bible Story project. It was a heady time! The research team scoured bookstores, purchasing numerous books of Bible stories. It scrutinized the artwork. It tried to ascertain strengths and weaknesses. The team visited museums featuring exhibits of ancient Near Eastern civilizations. Gradually a concept of an entirely different set of books began to jell—a series of books with appeal for the entire family.

The researchers decided that the main story should have a consistent fifth-grade reading level. They concluded that each story should be splendidly illustrated and that illustrations should have captions containing information not found in the story itself. The illustrations would include maps and photographs. Every element would support the intuition that the Bible stories talk about real people who did real exploits in real places.

The team felt it would be important to include a time line so that readers could see when these stories happened in connection with historical events in both the ancient Near East and other parts of the world. In some instances a certain element of the story—such as the stone David put into his sling when he killed Goliath—begged for explanation. What were sling stones? Thus the boxed explanations (labeled "Did You Know?") about this or that particular object, person, place, or custom.

The researchers thought it important to include the biblical text (in a version children could readily understand) with each story. And each story would be presented in two versions—a longer one at a fifth-grade reading level and a shorter one for tiny tots.

OPENING BLACK & WHITE DRAWING
Every story will open with a delightful little black-and-white pencil drawing by Darrel Tank.

THE BIBLE STORIES
These Bible stories for school-age children were especially written for this new series by Ruth Redding Brand. The stories are all written at a fifth-grade reading level and are designed to be read by children ages 9 through 12.

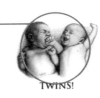

PHOTOGRAPHS

These photos of modern sites in Bible lands tie the stories to the same Holy Land that children see on the news each evening.

THE BIBLE TEXT

At the bottom of the second spread of each story are the actual Bible verses (from the IBC) on which the story is based. We put them at the bottom of the page because they are the foundation on which the whole series of books is based.

STORIES FOR PRESCHOOLERS

These delightful little one-page stories are actually condensed versions of the longer story—written for preschoolers, ages 2-5, and using simple language to retell the same Bible story for little ones.

But would such a product appeal to the market? So the publisher spent thousands of dollars for focus groups. You know what focus groups are, right? People are hired to spend an hour or so sitting around a table as they are introduced to samples of various kinds—"interventions," they're called. The coordinator asks questions to draw out respondents' feelings. Behind a large one-way window, observers take note of the respondents' suggestions and reactions.

Participants shared their likes and dislikes regarding such varied components as type font, page size, color tones, readability level, illustration styles, hardcover versus paperback, dust jackets, retail cost, etc. The results were reviewed and the proposed product tweaked further.

The publishing house next tested a pool of authors who were paid to write the same two Bible stories. Readers evaluated the submissions. Each story was ranked according to readers' responses. Finally, an author for the stories was selected—Ruth Redding Brand, a New England teacher and writer. The Review and Herald paid Brand for each story, and writing them became her full-time job for nearly eight years.

Once Brand had written and polished a story, she submitted it to the publishing house. Each story was critiqued for readability and literary quality. At least one biblical scholar reviewed every story for accuracy—and gave the publisher copious notes. Even a group of children critiqued each story.

After a few months the publisher sent Brand on an all-expenses-paid tour of the Holy Land. She, editor Gerald Wheeler, and researcher/photographer Gail Hunt chose as tour guide the world-renowned archaeologist Siegfried Horn (since deceased). They walked the dusty streets of Palestine, visited archaeological digs, and enjoyed the Sea of Galilee and the Jordan River. And Horn told them fascinating stories about life in the ancient Near East.

Because Brand wanted the stories to sound as dramatic as they actually were when they originally happened, she has occasionally taken literary license, sometimes providing dialogue not found in Scripture. She was careful, however, so that the added conversation was in keeping with the details recorded in the Bible.

Infrequently Brand also placed an invented character or two within a story. She gave them names and portrayed them talking to others who are named in the scriptural accounts. Why? Because sometimes the biblical account is so condensed it needs expansion to make the point inherent in the story obvious to us today. We will tell you when this happens in Brand's narratives.

One more explanation may be in order. Just as Brand sometimes created dialogue and additional characters, so also once in a while she has added an extra event—to help smooth transitions or to round out the story line.

We think you'll find Brand's imaginative efforts in harmony with the overall biblical emphasis. Every story comes directly from the Bible and is true to the spirit of the original text. They remain truth-filled stories, including the creative embellishments.

The Review and Herald contracted with other authors to write the Bible-based bedtime stories and the time lines. A photographer was about to find "models" in the crowded shopping malls around Washington, D.C., and Baltimore for our illustrators, but then the bottom dropped out. New management took over, and interest in the Family Bible Story project disappeared. Brand continued to write the stories, but all other contracts were declared null and void. The research was put into file folders and boxed up.

Several years elapsed. Those who had invested so much time in the project tried to convince management to resurrect the project. The publisher even hired marketing specialists (Haddock and Associates) from New York City to review our proposals. It looked as though the project might revive. But soon it was killed—again!

Once more new management took over, who became convinced to spend several more thousand dollars to redesign a single story—that of David and Goliath—to show to potential publishers around the world. Laura Stutzman, a skilled illustrator, prepared three paintings. She sewed costumes for Goliath and David and posed neighbors and friends while her husband (who later designed the Elvis Presley postage stamp) photographed them.

Designers prepared new layouts for the story. Hopes soared—once again. Only to be dashed during the autumn of 2000. Again boxes were crammed with research materials and once more archived.

Then in 2001 a new president joined the Review and Herald—Robert S. Smith. He had heard in past years about the project but had no solid knowledge about it. So he was introduced to the newly illustrated story of David and Goliath. He was impressed. About the same time the publisher's chief financial officer, Hepsiba S. Singh, began nudging us to publish at least some of the stories. The vice president of the Book Division, Mark B. Thomas, also showed renewed interest in the project. The Administrative Committee set up an ad hoc task force to put together a proposal.

And the results are now in your hands. We think you and your family will love this book (and others to appear in the near future) and will return to them again and again. Thank you for purchasing this book. It was prepared with many prayers that people like you, with children such as you have, would find the product interesting, informative, and spiritually stimulating.

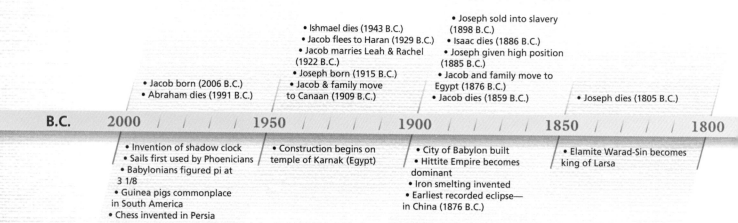

B.C. 2000 / / / / 1950 / / / / 1900 / / / / 1850 / / / / 1800

- Jacob born (2006 B.C.)
- Abraham dies (1991 B.C.)

- Ishmael dies (1943 B.C.)
- Jacob flees to Haran (1929 B.C.)
- Jacob marries Leah & Rachel (1922 B.C.)
- Joseph born (1915 B.C.)
- Jacob & family move to Canaan (1909 B.C.)

- Joseph sold into slavery (1898 B.C.)
- Isaac dies (1886 B.C.)
- Joseph given high position (1885 B.C.)
- Jacob and family move to Egypt (1876 B.C.)
- Jacob dies (1859 B.C.)

- Joseph dies (1805 B.C.)

- Invention of shadow clock
- Sails first used by Phoenicians
- Babylonians figured pi at 3 1/8
- Guinea pigs commonplace in South America
- Chess invented in Persia

- Construction begins on temple of Karnak (Egypt)

- City of Babylon built
- Hittite Empire becomes dominant
- Iron smelting invented
- Earliest recorded eclipse— in China (1876 B.C.)

- Elamite Warad-Sin becomes king of Larsa

JACOB/ISRAEL

Jacob, son of Isaac and Rebekah and twin of Esau, was later renamed Israel. He herded flocks. Jacob was 77 years old when he fled to Uncle Laban in Haran after cheating Esau. Jacob fathered 12 sons and one daughter. When he was 130 years old, Jacob moved to Egypt, where Joseph, his long-lost son, was vizier. He died at age 147.

ESAU/EDOM

Esau was Jacob's twin brother. He also went by the name Edom. Esau liked to hunt. He had five sons. When the family thought that Isaac was on his deathbed (he wasn't), Jacob subversively obtained Esau's blessing. Esau vowed to murder Jacob. Twenty years later Jacob met Esau and discovered that Esau had forgiven him.

RACHEL

Rachel was Laban's daughter. In order to win her hand in marriage, Jacob served Laban for seven years. To Jacob the time sped by because he'd fallen so madly in love. Laban tricked Jacob on the wedding day, giving him Leah, Rachel's older sister, instead of Rachel herself. At first Rachel could not conceive but finally gave birth to Joseph and Benjamin.

LEAH

Leah means "wild cow" or "gazelle." Laban tricked Jacob into marrying her when he (Jacob) thought he was really marrying Rachel. Leah and Jacob had six sons (Reuben, Simeon, Levi, Judah, Issachar, and Zebulun) and one daughter (Dinah). Her maidservant was Zilpah, whom her father gave to her as a wedding present.

"Surely the Lord is in this place; and I knew it not."

Genesis 28:16

ISAAC AND REBEKAH

At Eliezer's soft command, the weary camels sank to their knees. They had walked 500 miles from Hebron to the city of Nahor in northern Mesopotamia.

Eliezer was tired too. He settled himself under a tree where he could watch the girls as they came to the well in late afternoon. If the Lord willed, one of these young women swinging down the path, water jar on her shoulder, would become Isaac's wife.

Abraham had said firmly, "Don't get a wife . . . from the Canaanite girls. . . . Instead, go back . . . to the land of my relatives. Get a wife for my son Isaac from there."[1]

Now the girls were coming into view. Eliezer prayed, "I will say to one of the girls, 'Please put your jar down so I can drink.' Then let her say, 'Drink, and I will also give water to your camels.' If that happens, I will know she is the right one."[2]

<hr />

Rebekah hummed a tune as she descended the damp stone steps to the spring. She brought the goatskin bucket, streaming with water, up from the pool of water.

Eliezer stepped forward. She could tell from his tired and dusty looks that he had been traveling. She could see the 10 camels kneeling nearby, burdened with all kinds of supplies.

"Please give me a little water from your jar."

"Drink, sir!" she answered as she poured water from her pitcher into his flask.

Eliezer drank deeply, but his mind raced ahead. The girl was kind. She was beautiful. But was she the *right* girl? Eliezer remembered his prayer. If she offered to draw water for his camels . . .

As he finished drinking, his heart pounded—would she turn now and walk away? Rebekah lifted the jar to her shoulder, smiled, and offered, "I will also pour some water for your camels."[3]

Eliezer let out his breath in one big burst and realized he hadn't breathed ever since that last swallow of water!

Rebekah hurried to the wooden watering trough and emptied her jar into it. The water spilled along the bottom of the long trough, barely wetting it. She turned and ran down the stone steps again. She lowered the bucket again. Up it came, full of sloshing water. She ran to the trough. Again and again and again Rebekah ran to the well and back again to the watering trough. At last the trough was full.

Eliezer tapped the first kneeling camel. It rose jerkily to its feet and walked on its knobby-kneed legs to the watering trough. Others followed it. *Slurp—slurp—slurp!* The water was gone! The camels looked at Eliezer and Rebekah from under their heavy lids as if to say, Is that all there is?

Rebekah was already on her way back to the well, bringing more water, more water, more water.

Eliezer watched in wonder as Rebekah ran back and forth, without complaint, to water a stranger's camels. He felt sure this girl must be the one the Lord had chosen for Isaac.

From the folds of his robe Eliezer drew some expensive jewelry, gifts from Abraham. "These are for you," Eliezer said gratefully.

Rebekah's eyes grew wide. "Why—thank you!"

"Tell me," Eliezer went on, "who is your father? Is there a place in his house for me and my men to spend the night?" He held his breath again. Could this girl possibly be from Abraham's brother's family?

"My father is Bethuel. He is the son of Milcah and Nahor." (Eliezer nearly shouted for joy!) "Yes, we have straw for your camels. We have a place for you to spend the night."

"Blessed is the Lord, the God of my master Abraham," Eliezer exclaimed.[4]

GOOD NEWS

Rebekah ran as fast as she could back to her family, forgetting Eliezer, who was still standing by the well. Her family listened, openmouthed, as she told of her experience. The eyes of her brother, Laban, quickly caught the glint of Rebekah's gold ring and bracelets, and he hurried to the well.

"You are welcome to come in. . . . I have prepared the house for you and also a place for your camels."[5]

As Eliezer made his way with Laban to the home of Bethuel, all Rebekah's family buzzed with excitement. "Welcome!" everyone cried as Eliezer entered. "Please have something to eat!"

Eliezer, however, had more important things on his mind than eating. "I am Abraham's servant . . ." he began.[6] Leaving out no detail, Eliezer told of Abraham's instructions to find a wife in Nahor's family for Isaac. He told how God had led him to

GENESIS 24:2-67

Abraham called [his oldest] servant to him and said, . . . "Go back to my country. . . . Get a wife for . . . Isaac." . . . [The servant] went to . . . Nahor's city. . . .

The servant said, "Lord, you are the God of my master. . . . Allow me to find a wife for [Isaac]. . . . The girls from the city are coming out to get water. I will say to one of the girls, 'Please put your jar down so I can drink.' . . . Let her say, 'Drink, and I will also give water to your camels.' If that happens, I will know she is the right one." . . .

Rebekah came out of the city. . . . She went down to the spring. . . . The servant . . . said, "Please give me a little water. . . ."

Rebekah said, "Drink." . . . "I will also pour some water for your camels." . . .

The servant asked, "Who is your father? Is there a place in his house for me and my

The oldest houses archaeologists have found are from Mesopotamia. During the fourth millennium B.C. Mesopotamians invented courtyard houses, in which rooms were located on the perimeter of a common area.

Rebekah. Then he asked Rebekah's family if they were willing for her to be Isaac's wife.

Rebekah's father and brother answered quickly. "This is clearly from the Lord. . . . Let her marry your master's son."[7]

Eliezer thanked God again and gave presents to Rebekah's whole family. They chattered happily as they examined the gifts from Abraham.

Then they looked at Rebekah. Realizing they would be losing her, Rebekah's mother and brother said, "Let Rebekah stay with us at least ten days. After that she may go."

Eliezer replied, "Do not make me wait."

"We will call Rebekah and ask her what she wants to do."

Rebekah came into the room and listened as the

men to spend the night?"

Rebekah answered, ". . . We have a place for you to spend the night." . . .

She had a brother named Laban. . . . Laban said, ". . . I have prepared the house for you." . . .

But the servant said, "I will not eat until I have told you why I came." . . .

Laban and Bethuel answered, "This is clearly from the Lord. . . . Rebekah is yours. . . . Let her marry your master's son." . . .

Rebekah and her servant girls got on the camels and followed the servant. . . .

One evening [Isaac] went out to the field

to think. As he looked up, he saw camels coming. . . . [Rebekah] asked . . . , "Who is that man . . . ?" The servant answered, "That is my master." So Rebekah covered her face. . . . Isaac brought Rebekah into the tent of Sarah. . . . And she became his wife.

family explained what they wanted her to do. Her eyes misted as she thought of how much she would miss her mother and her family, but she knew that God had chosen her to be Isaac's wife. Although she had never seen Isaac, Rebekah felt honored to be part of God's miracle.

"Do you want to go with this man now?"

"Yes, I do."[8]

The next morning, as Rebekah, her special servant Deborah, her other maids, Eliezer, and the other men from Abraham's household prepared to leave, Rebekah's family said a special blessing for her.

Isaac paced back and forth, back and forth. An occasional raven winged its way across the blue sky. But Isaac's mind was not on the blue sky, the green grass, the prickly thistles in the field, or the squawking ravens.

Many weeks had passed since Eliezer had left. Isaac wondered, *Has a girl from my father's relatives been willing to leave her family and travel 500 miles to Canaan to marry a man she has never seen?*

Then in the distance Isaac saw bumps that

moved—camels—black against the brilliant sun. He shaded his eyes and squinted. Bigger and bigger the camels grew, and then he saw people—some riding, some walking. Excitement hammered in his chest, and he ran to meet the caravan.

Rebekah spotted Isaac running toward their caravan. Good manners compelled her, in the presence of a strange man, to dismount. As she slid from the camel, she veiled her face.

Isaac came closer. Now he could clearly see . . . yes, it was Eliezer! And he could see the woman who now stood before him, her face veiled except for her large, dark eyes.

Isaac led her to his tent. There he told Rebekah about Sarah. He told her about the miracle of his own birth. He explained that God had pledged that he, as Abraham's promised son, would have children whom God would bless. He pointed out that she would be the mother of those children.

Rebekah listened intently. She liked

this quiet man. A song started in her heart. And the Bible says that she became Isaac's wife and that he "loved her very much."[9]

[1]Genesis 24:3, 4, ICB.
[2]Verse 14, ICB.
[3]Verses 17-19, ICB.
[4]Verses 23-27, ICB.
[5]Verse 31, ICB.
[6]Verse 34, ICB.
[7]Verses 50, 51, ICB.
[8]Verses 55-58, ICB.
[9]Verse 66, ICB.

Isaac and Rebekah

Isaac grew up to be a handsome man.

"Isaac must marry a good wife," Abraham told his servant Eliezer one day. "But no women here worship God. I want you to make the long trip back to my old country," Abraham continued. "There you will find a good woman for Isaac."

"How?" Eliezer asked.

"God will help you."

Eliezer rode on a camel for 500 miles. When Eliezer was near Abraham's old city, he began to pray: "Dear God, please choose the right girl for Isaac. I will say to the girls, 'Please give me a drink of water.' When the best girl comes, have her offer to get water for all my camels."

Eliezer stopped by a wellspring. Many girls were getting water. Finally Eliezer saw a beautiful girl at the well.

"Please give me a drink," Eliezer said.

The girl smiled. "Yes, sir," she answered.

Eliezer took a deep drink and waited.

"I am Rebekah," the girl said, "and I will carry water for your camels." She hurried to the well and worked very hard until all the camels had their fill of water.

God showed me the right girl! Eliezer thought happily. He gave Rebekah some gifts.

Rebekah raced home to tell her family about the stranger at the well.

Rebekah's family invited Eliezer to their home. Soon they discovered they were related to Abraham.

"This is wonderful," Eliezer said. "God has found the perfect wife for Isaac."

Rebekah's family was excited. Rebekah was excited too. She would miss her family when she left them, but she was pleased to serve God.

It was a long trip back to Abraham and Isaac's home, but Rebekah was happy to meet Isaac. They were married, and loved each other very much.

—HEATHER GROVET

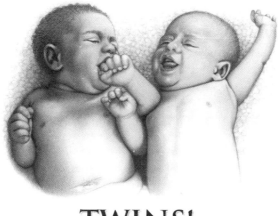

TWINS!

Rebekah absentmindedly twirled one silky strand of hair round and round her finger.

"Isaac, why do you suppose we have not yet had a child? God promised us children, but we've been married for 19 years!" She wanted to say more, but found no words to express her longing for a baby or her confusion about God's promises.

Nineteen years! It seemed impossible that so much time had gone by since she had left her family in the small city of Nahor and moved to Canaan so she could become Isaac's wife. But, she thought quickly, she would do it all again for the quiet, gentle man who was her husband, and for the wonderful God he worshipped. But why did other women have babies so easily, while she, to whom God had promised children, went year after year with empty arms?

Three deep creases—straight up and down—appeared between Isaac's eyebrows. Those three lines appeared every time he thought hard about a problem. At last he answered, "I remember Mother and Father telling me of their long wait for a child. Years passed before God even promised that they would have a son, then 25 more years passed before that promise was fulfilled! Mother was 90 years old when I was born! Everyone knew that God had performed a miracle.

"I hope we don't have to wait that long, Rebekah, but I do know that we can

depend on God to keep His promise."

As Rebekah ground flour between two flat stones, her mind worked in rhythm with her hands. "God keeps His word. God keeps His word," she kept repeating to herself.

Suddenly Isaac stood at her elbow. "Rebekah, I need to talk to God. I may be gone awhile."

Isaac smiled, but Rebekah noticed those three deep lines between his eyebrows. *He's going to build an altar. He's going to ask God to give us a child,* she thought to herself. Aloud, she said, "Take your time, Isaac. Don't hurry. When you come back I'll have fresh bread and stew for you!"

Later, as she peeled the fresh, flat cakes of bread from the hot stove, Rebekah looked up to see Isaac striding toward her, a big smile on his face. The lines between his eyebrows had disappeared.

God will answer our prayers! Rebekah smiled to herself.

In the weeks to come Rebekah came to realize that she carried brand-new life within her body. But as the weeks passed, she felt that something was wrong. The baby moved so much inside her, she felt as though her baby was fighting with someone! What was wrong? Was her baby all right?

Troubled, she left her tent and the chatter of the servants and headed for the peace and quiet of the grain fields. As she sank to her knees on the sunbaked earth, the golden grain skimmed her cheeks and welcomed her into a private little world where she could talk out loud to God.

As she told God her worries, His voice suddenly filled the silence. Rebekah listened in wonder as He spoke to her. "Don't worry, Rebekah. Everything is all right. Two nations are in your body. Two groups of people will be taken from you. One group will be stronger than the other. The older will serve the younger."*

The Negev, where Isaac lived, is some 5,000 square miles of desert in Palestine. It forms part of the great Saharo-Arabian desert belt.

GENESIS 25:19-26

This is the family history of Isaac. Abraham had a son named Isaac. When Isaac was 40 years old, he married Rebekah. Rebekah was from Northwest Mesopotamia. She was Bethuel's daughter and the sister of Laban the Aramean. Isaac's wife could not have children. So Isaac prayed to the Lord for her. The Lord heard Isaac's prayer, and Rebekah became pregnant.

While she was pregnant, the babies struggled inside her. She asked, "Why is this happening to me?" Then she went to get an answer from the Lord.

Children, especially boys, were considered valuable resources in the ancient Near East. However, the infant mortality rate was high—as was the death of mothers during childbirth. The birth of a child was seen as a gift from God.

Rebekah whispered, "Thank You, God!" and ran back to the tent to tell Isaac.

Weeks later strange shadows on the walls of the tent flickered as Rebekah's servants held small oil lamps around her mat. The time had come for not just one baby, but two little boys, to be born.

The midwife bending over Rebekah suddenly straightened and placed a wiggling tiny form into

The Lord said to her, "Two nations are in your body. Two groups of people will be taken from you. One group will be stronger than the other. The older will serve the younger."

And when the time came, Rebekah gave birth to twins. The first baby was born red. His skin was like a hairy robe. So he was named Esau. When the second baby was born, he was holding on to Esau's heel.

So that baby was named Jacob. Isaac was 60 years old when they were born.

PROPER NAMES
IN THE ANCIENT NEAR EAST

In the ancient Near East names were not just groups of sounds to identify a person or place. When you learned a name, often you also had an important clue to its bearer's traits or even future destiny. Or you might discover the beliefs and hopes of those who bestowed the name.

A name might indicate an obvious characteristic. When Isaac and Rebekah had their first-born, they named him Esau ("hairy") (Genesis 25:25). His twin brother, Jacob ("heel grab-ber"), received his name because he was grabbing Esau's heel at birth (Genesis 25:26). The name foreshad-owed Jacob's personality and behav-ior. He stole Esau's birthright and later tricked his father-in-law, Laban, out of much of his wealth.

The town Gibeah ("hill") received its name for its topo-graphical position. Bethlehem ("house of bread") alludes to the region's ability to grow grain. Jacob named one spot Bethel ("house of God"), because God had revealed His presence there (Genesis 28:12-15). Engedi means "spring of the goat" because of the wild goats that lived there.

Other names might indicate personality traits or habits. Deborah ("honeybee") aptly describes the busy woman who was judge, prophet, wife, mother, warrior, and singer. Nabal ("fool") captures his attitude toward life. Even his wife had to admit that "folly is with him" (1 Samuel 25:25).

Often a name indicated the religious beliefs of the parent, and what deity he or she worshipped. The prophet Obadiah's name means "God's servant." Many Old Testament names incorporate one of the Hebrew names of God, most frequently El or Yah or Yahu, short forms of Yahweh. Typical names include: Eliashib: "God restores"; Elijah: "Yahweh is my God"; Elimelech: "God is king"; Jehoshaphat: "Yahweh has judged"; Zechariah: "Yahweh has remembered." Sometimes the name of God would only be implied. Baruch ("blessed") stood for "God has blessed."

Other names indicated a parent's thankfulness: Mattaniah ("gift of Yahweh"), Elnathan ("God has given [this child]"), and Shemaiah ("Yahweh has heard [the parent's prayer]"). The name given to a child might reflect the parent's aspirations for the child: Jeberechiah: "May Yahweh bless [this child]"; Ezekiel: "May God strengthen [this child]"; Jehiel: "May God preserve [this child]."

But her words stopped short as another baby made its way into the circle of light in the dark tent. "This one held his brother by the heel!" chuckled the midwife as she placed the second baby in the crook of Rebekah's other arm. "He just grabbed that heel like it was something that belonged to him!" So Rebekah called him Jacob, which means "heel grabber" in Hebrew.

Of course, the two newborn babies didn't care what their names were or that a circle of admirers examined them in the lamplight. They didn't know that God had special plans for them or how much their parents loved them. Nor did they know that great troubles lay ahead for them.

Tiny Jacob stuffed his fist into his mouth.

Rebekah's waiting arms. The baby wailed. Rebekah smiled as she examined the little red body, all covered with dark fuzz. "Oh, look at my little hairy baby!" she exclaimed. "I'll name him Esau because he has so much hair!"

Esau yawned, a big pink yawn. Rebekah smiled con-tentedly. "Please go get Isaac!" she directed a servant. "He must see the sons that the Lord has given us!"

*Genesis 25:23, ICB.

Twins!

Isaac and Rebekah loved each other very much. Life was good except for one thing. They had no children.

"We have been married 19 years!" Rebekah complained. "I wonder why God has not given us any children."

Isaac looked serious. "I do not know," he said, "but we need to keep trusting God."

Isaac went outside to the fields to pray while Rebekah cooked the next meal. When Isaac returned, a big smile covered his face!

"God told me that soon we will have a baby!" Isaac shouted.

Before long Rebekah became pregnant.

"I am so happy!" Rebekah sang. But as the months passed, Rebekah began to feel terrible.

One day Rebekah bowed her head and prayed. "Dear God, I can't stand this! The baby inside me is moving too much. Something must be wrong. What should I do?"

God said, "Rebekah, you are carrying two babies. One will be stronger than the other, and the older one will serve the younger one."

"Thank You, God," Rebekah whispered.

Soon the time came for the babies to be born.

"It's a boy!" the midwife said, holding the first baby up to show Rebekah.

"Isn't he cute!" Rebekah smiled. "He has so much red hair that it looks like he's wearing a fur coat!"

So they named the first little boy Esau, which means "hairy."

Then the other twin was born. "This one held his older brother by the heel," the midwife laughed. "He grabbed it tight."

So Rebekah named the second baby Jacob, which meant "heel grabber" in their language!

Isaac and Rebekah were filled with joy. God had given them not one but two little boys to love. Now they would need to wait and see God's plan for their family.

—HEATHER GROVET

HIGH-PRICED SOUP

Esau pushed up the sleeve of his tunic and flexed his muscle. "Hey, Jacob! Look at that!" he shouted as his muscle bulged on his hairy arm.

"Uh-huh," Jacob responded, barely glancing at his brother.

Jacob was lying on his back, looking at clouds. That big fluffy one looked just like a sheep in his father's flocks, the one that had just given birth to twin lambs—one white, one black. And that cloud, the shiny one with the sun behind it, looked almost like an angel! Jacob, of course, had never seen an angel, but Father Isaac had told him stories of the Garden of Eden. And Jacob imagined that an angel must look shiny and glowing like that towering white cloud.

"Boys! Come here!" Rebekah's voice put an end to Jacob's daydreaming and Esau's muscle flexing.

Rebekah shaded her eyes with her hand as she watched the twins come running. *Were ever twins more different than Esau and Jacob?* she wondered. Esau, big-boned, husky, hairy, bursting with noisy life, could never be still. He stalked life just as he stalked wild game with his bow and arrow. When he wanted something, he rushed upon it, never thinking of the consequences.

Jacob, slender and graceful, was the quiet one. He loved to dream and think big

thoughts. But despite his daydreaming, he was always dependable. *Jacob may have his head in the clouds, but his feet are on the ground,* Rebekah told herself.

The boys reached her, panting. Esau's black eyes sparkled from the exercise. Jacob's cheeks glowed as he ran his fingers through his wavy hair.

"Your father has something important to tell you." Rebekah bit her lip to keep from saying more. She knew that Isaac intended to explain the birthright to the boys, but especially to Esau, in more detail than he had ever done before. She remembered, more clearly than she remembered anything else that had ever happened to her, God's words: "Your older son will serve the younger."

Why had she never been able to make Isaac understand that? Of course—he had not heard God's words to her.

Now as the twins each picked a stone to sit on while Isaac talked to them, Rebekah listened.

"The birthright," Isaac began, looking at Esau, "is the most important gift and responsibility a father can give to his son—his oldest son," he emphasized as he spotted Rebekah looking on and saw her disapproving look.

"When you receive the birthright," he continued, "you will own twice as much—a double portion of my land and flocks and servants. But much more

important than that, you will become the head of the family. You will see that everyone in our family marries within the tribe of Abraham, my father, so that the worship of the only true God will continue. You must take good care of the servants and their families. And you must keep on offering sacrifices to God as my father, Abraham, did. You, to whom I give the birthright, will enjoy a special relationship with Him."

Jacob edged forward on his rock, eyes shining. The birthright! To have God's special blessing, to offer the sacrifices for his family, perhaps even to talk with God as his grandfather Abraham had done—! *I wish that birthright could be mine!* he thought to himself.

Esau shifted uncomfortably, the rock under him feeling harder by the minute. It seemed that his father would never stop talking!

Rebekah, through narrowed eyes, noted Jacob's eagerness and Esau's restlessness. *I'm going to tell Jacob that he is the one God has chosen to receive the birthright!* she decided. *If easygoing Isaac won't listen to me, I'll have to take things into my own hands!*

In the weeks and years to come Jacob thought about the birthright and the amazing news his mother had told him. The birthright would belong to him! But how was he to get it from Esau?

> ## "THE BIRTHRIGHT IS THE MOST IMPORTANT GIFT AND RESPONSIBILITY A FATHER CAN GIVE TO HIS SON—HIS OLDEST SON."

GENESIS 25:27-34

When the boys grew up, Esau became a skilled hunter. He loved to be out in the fields. But Jacob was a quiet man. He stayed among the tents. Isaac loved Esau. Esau hunted the wild animals that Isaac enjoyed eating. But Rebekah loved Jacob.

One day Jacob was boiling a pot of vegetable soup. Esau came in from hunting in the fields. He was weak from hunger. So Esau said to Jacob, "Let me eat some of that red soup. I am weak with hunger." (That is why people call him Edom.)

But Jacob said, "You must sell me your

"What would you take for the birthright?" Jacob asked one day.

"What do you want that for?" Esau paused, a smirk on his face. "If I ever get ready to sell it, I'll let you know!" Jacob's face flamed. How could his brother joke about something that meant so much?

"Here!" Esau dropped the ibex at the feet of Jacob, who was slowly stirring a bubbling stew. "I'll be back later to season it the way Father likes it."

Isaac rounded the corner of the tent just in time

At first, hunting in the ancient Near East was not a sport. It was the way to get food. According to some sources, bows and arrows were used as early as the Stone Age.

to catch the end of the conversation. He smiled fondly as he looked at Esau. Esau still held his bow, while his wooden, flint-tipped arrows hung from his shoulder.

"I see you had another successful hunt," Isaac said.

"Yes, Father. I've killed an ibex. You'll have it for supper!"

Jacob kept stirring his stew. The simmering vegetables swam in slow circles, round and round the pot. His thoughts seemed to follow them, round and round, with no place to go. How could he get the birthright from Esau? Father would never permit it!

Years dragged by. On a spring morning when even the desert around Esau and Jacob's home blossomed with oleander and mountain tulips and fields of white crocuses, Esau picked up his bow and left to hunt.

Esau breathed deeply of the early-morning air as with long strides he headed into the dry riverbeds and their surrounding bushes. As usual, the excitement of the hunt flowed through him, and he eagerly scanned the water holes for telltale movement. An ibex, perhaps a gazelle, might step, unsuspecting, from the brush. Esau's strong fingers would fit an arrow to

rights as the firstborn son."

Esau said, "I am almost dead from hunger. If I die, all of my father's wealth will not help me."

But Jacob said, "First, promise me that you will give it to me." So Esau made a promise to Jacob. In this way he sold his part of their father's wealth to Jacob. Then Jacob gave Esau bread and vegetable soup. Esau ate and drank and then left. So Esau showed how little he cared about his rights as the firstborn son.

COOKING IN THE ANCIENT NEAR EAST

the bow and pull, and once again he would know the thrill of mastery!

But the sun climbed high in the sky, and the birdsongs faded in the sultry air. The animals seemed to have melted into the hills. Once Esau spotted an ibex as it looked at him with startled eyes, but even as his arrow sped toward its target, the animal leaped into the cover of reeds and disappeared. Esau wiped the sweat from his forehead. He took a few gulps of water from his flask, paying no attention to the water that dribbled from his chin and chest. What a wasted morning! He couldn't remember a day when the animals had been so scarce! Removing the cloth wrapping from a hunk of cheese he carried with him, he greedily stuffed the strong-smelling food into his mouth. He chewed, swallowed hard, and washed his meal down with more water. Springing to his feet, he grabbed his bow with new determination. "I'll go

People in Old Testament times had to grow, store, and cook their own food. Dependent on their homegrown crops, most ancient people were just one harvest away from starvation.

The main food was flat (pita) bread made from wheat, barley, millet, or spelt emmer flour. Each day the women would grind enough grain for the day's baking. People also roasted grains, eating them either whole or crushed.

Next in importance were fruits, vegetables, and dairy products. The most common fruits were grapes, figs, dates, apples (or quince), melons, and pomegranates. Grapes, figs, and dates could be dried and pressed into flat cakes. Vegetables consisted of beans, red and white lentils, chickpeas, cucumbers, leeks, onions, garlic, and wild roots. Olives produced oil for cooking and fuel for lamps. Sheep and goats provided milk for cheese, curds, and butter. Spices and herbs served as flavorings. Honey, grape, or date syrup could sweeten the food.

Meat was too expensive except for special occasions. Because they had no refrigeration, people had to eat meat as soon as it was slaughtered. When families killed a fatted calf or sheep for some celebration, they would invite friends and neighbors to share it so that nothing was wasted. Otherwise people rarely used

meat except as a flavoring. The flocks and herds were a source of wealth. To eat any of the livestock was like withdrawing one's savings or cashing in certificates of deposit, stocks, or bonds so that one could pay for eating in a restaurant.

Drinking water was scarce and had to be carried from a spring or well. People later dug cisterns to collect the winter rainfall. Wine was the other main drink. The ancients often heavily diluted it with water. If it was already fermented, the slight amount of alcohol would kill some of the microorganisms always present in the water.

Besides bread, the main item in the meal was a stew thick enough to be dipped out with pieces of bread. Jacob cooked himself a lentil stew that Esau traded his birthright for. Both vegetables and meat were boiled in cooking pots over an open fire.

Pomegranates provided tasty food and juice.

outside the thickets," he muttered. "The sheep must be hiding among the rocks."

Back home, Jacob crouched before a steaming stewpot, stirring its thick contents. But his eyes were on the evening sky as the dying sun threw red and purple streamers across it. Red lentils, tasty and tender, bubbled in the pot. Absentmindedly Jacob threw some garlic, onion, and cumin into the pot and continued stirring.

Esau is late returning from the hunt, Jacob mused. Then suddenly Esau appeared. No lifeless animal rode across his shoulders, but he staggered a bit because he was so tired. "What's in the pot?" he asked, slumping to the ground. "I'm starved!"

Jacob's heart pounded with the possibility his mind suggested. But his gaze and voice were cool and level as he asked, "Just how hungry *are* you, Esau?"

"How hungry am I? I've climbed over and around a million rocks, stumbled through brush and thistles, followed a gazelle for miles, and then lost it. All I've had to eat is a piece of cheese! And you ask how hungry I am! If you don't give me some of that stew right now, I'll die!"

"Perhaps," continued Jacob, "you're hungry enough to make a trade?"

"What do you want? I'll give you anything!"

Jacob's eyes burned into his brother's. "You must sell me your rights as the firstborn son."[1]

Esau threw back his shaggy head and laughed. "Is *that* all? The *birthright*? What good is a birthright to a starving man? If I die, all of my father's wealth will not help me."[2] But Jacob was not yet satisfied. "First, promise me that you will give it to me."[3]

"OK!" Esau yelled. "I solemnly swear by the God of our father Isaac that the birthright is yours."

Esau scooped up the thick stew with a piece of flat bread and stuffed it into his mouth. Before he had finished chewing or swallowing, he stuffed in another mouthful. When his bowl was empty, he asked for more. Jacob happily refilled it.

Rebekah, watching and listening from the entrance to her tent, had missed nothing. She smiled triumphantly. The birthright would be Jacob's, just as God had promised!

Suddenly Jacob turned, and a look of pleased understanding flashed between mother and son.

But a problem remained. How would Jacob convince his father to pronounce on him the special, unchangeable blessing due the firstborn son?

Both sexes of the dorcas gazelle have horns. They can run steadily at 30 miles an hour. Some may never drink water, getting needed moisture from the plants they eat.

Brand has added some scenes, not mentioned in the Bible, to round out the story line. She has tried to be true to the personalities of the two boys and the geography of the region.

[1]Genesis 25:31, ICB.
[2]Verse 32, ICB.
[3]Verse 33, ICB.

High-priced Soup

"Jacob, let's go hunting!" Esau hollered. He held a bow in his strong, hairy hands.

Jacob shook his head. "I have other things to do."

"Sissy!" Esau said. "No wonder Father likes me best. I hunt for him."

"Who cares?" Jacob said. "Mother likes me best."

Esau stomped off angrily.

Jacob shrugged his shoulders and began making a tasty stew. *We're twins, but we're so different,* Jacob thought.

Jacob daydreamed as he stirred the stew. Just last week Father Isaac had announced that Esau would get the special family birthright. "The birthright is important," he had said. "It is for the oldest son."

"That's me," Esau yawned.

"Esau will get twice as much land and animals," Isaac had continued. "He will be responsible for our family, and he will have a special relationship with God."

I want the birthright, Jacob said to himself. *An angel told Mother I would get it. "The older son will serve the younger."*

Late in the afternoon while Jacob was eating his stew Esau hurried into the house. "I'm starving!" Esau yelled.

"What did you shoot?" Jacob asked.

"Nothing!" Esau groaned. "And I'll die if I don't eat soon. Give me some of that stew."

Jacob thought quickly. "I'll sell you some stew," he said.

"Sell?"

"Yes. You can pay for the stew by giving me your birthright."

"Fine!" Esau yelled. "What good is my birthright if I starve to death?"

"Do you promise?"

Esau dumped stew into a bowl. "I swear by God," he growled. "Now let me eat."

Jacob smiled. *This is great!* he thought. *Poor foolish Esau doesn't even know what has happened. Now all I need is Father's blessing for the firstborn.*

Esau burped and filled his bowl again.

But neither Jacob nor Esau had thought about God. Was this God's plan?

—HEATHER GROVET

REBEKAH'S SCHEME AND JACOB'S LIE

Judith clung to Esau's arm as a smile, half shy, half bold, lit up her features. In one hand she clutched the small bronze figure of a bull. On its back stood the storm god.

Isaac felt the blood pounding in his head. His son Esau had not asked for advice or even tried to find a wife from Abraham's many relatives back in Mesopotamia.

Isaac and Rebekah had little time to recover from their shock before Esau brought home another wife, Basemath, another local girl. Soon Judith's and Basemath's idols became common sights. Before long his children were worshipping the sun goddess and the storm god and the war god, but did not worship the God of Abraham and Isaac.

Isaac's eyesight was bad. Faces and objects blurred as he strained to discover who and what they were. Then he got sick. One day Isaac felt so weak he couldn't get out of bed. Overcome by a sense of dread, he wondered if he might die soon. "I must give my blessing to my son, my firstborn, Esau!" he moaned.

"Esau, Esau!" he called. Esau, ready to leave for the hunt, burst into his father's tent.

"I am old. I don't know when I might die. So take your bow and arrows, and go hunting. . . . Kill an animal for me to eat. Prepare the tasty food that I love. Bring it to me, and I will eat. Then I will bless you before I die."[1]

Rebekah overheard Isaac's words and froze. Jacob must have the blessing! God's

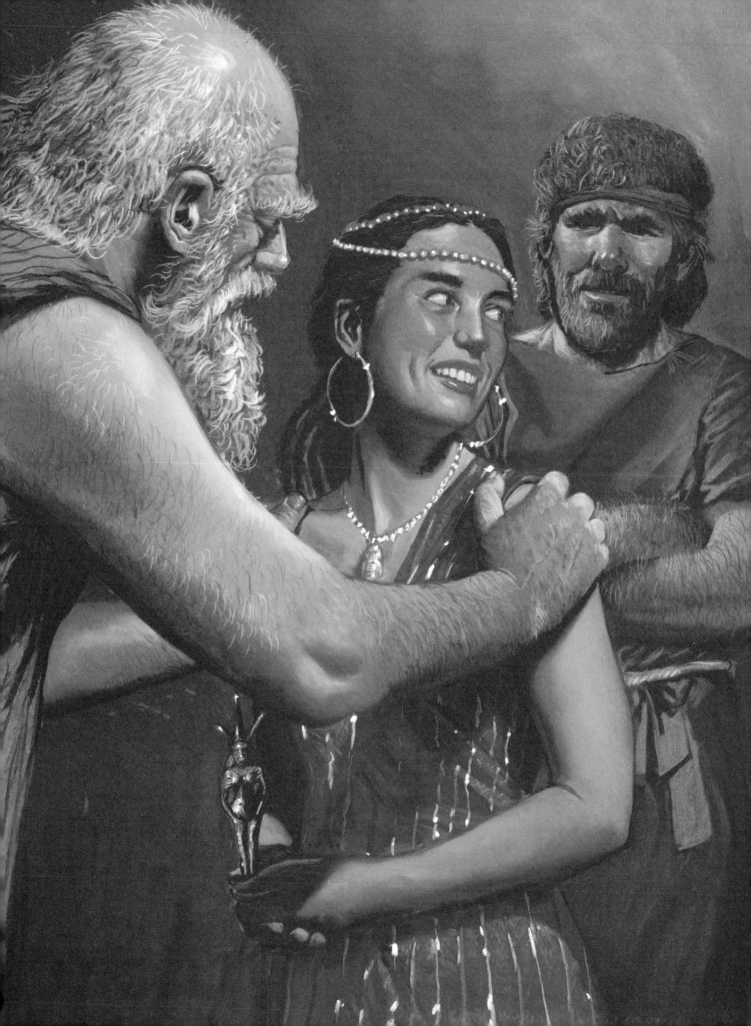

words pounded in her head, "The older will serve the younger," and Jacob was the "younger." And he served God, craved the blessing, wanted to lead his family in the worship of the Creator-God. But Esau with his headstrong nature and idol-worshipping wives cared nothing for the worship of the God of Abraham and Isaac! She must do something. Fast!

Quickly she slipped from the tent. Shading her eyes, she scanned the fields. *Jacob, where are you?* she cried silently. There, a figure among the sheep . . . Running toward the flock, Rebekah reached Jacob as his sensitive fingers rubbed and flexed the stiff leg of an injured sheep.

"Jacob!" Rebekah cried. "Listen, I heard your father talking to your brother Esau. Your father said, 'Kill an animal. Prepare some tasty food for me to eat. Then I will bless you before the Lord before I die.' . . . Do what I tell you. Go out to our goats and bring me two fat young ones. I will prepare them just the way your father likes them. Then you will take the food to your father. And he will bless you before he dies."[2]

"But they aren't wild game."

"Trust me. I'll fix them so he won't know the difference."

"Esau is a hairy man. I am smooth! If my father touches me, he will know I am not Esau. . . . He will place a curse on me because I tried to trick him."

"If your father puts a curse on you, I will accept the blame. Just do what I said," she insisted, with great motions of her arms.[3]

Jacob ran to obey, his thoughts spinning wildly. He must have the blessing! But did God want him to get it this way?

Jacob slaughtered two young goats. Rebekah prepared the meat. Then she handed him some of Esau's best clothes. They had Esau's distinct scent on them.

Jacob watched his mother's skillful fingers fashion a pair of long gloves from the black, silky, hairy goatskin. The gloves fit smoothly over his hands and arms. Then he sensed his mother's light, sure touch as she smoothed some more goatskin over the bare skin of his neck.

She placed in his hands a steaming bowl and fragrant bread. And urged him, "Go."

Breathing deeply, he shot a look at his mother that said, I'll do my best! And he entered his father's tent.

Jacob paused for a moment, allowing his eyes to adjust to the dim light of the tent. Isaac lay quietly, his face turned toward the tent wall, but as he heard Jacob's step, he half raised himself.

"Father!" Jacob began.

> **JACOB MUST HAVE THE BLESSING! GOD'S WORDS POUNDED IN REBEKAH'S HEAD, "THE OLDER WILL SERVE THE YOUNGER," AND JACOB WAS THE "YOUNGER."**

GENESIS 27:1-43

[Isaac's] eyes were not good. . . . He called . . . Esau to him. . . .

Isaac said, ". . . Take your bow and arrows, and go hunting. . . . Prepare the food . . . I love. Bring it to me. . . . I will bless you." . . .

Rebekah said to . . . Jacob, ". . . Bring me two [goats]. I will prepare them. . . . Take the food to your father. And he will bless you." . . .

Jacob said . . . , "Esau is . . . hairy. . . . Father . . . will know I am not Esau." . . .

[Rebekah] took the best clothes of . . . Esau. . . . She put them on . . . Jacob. She took the skins of the goats. And she put them on Jacob's hands and neck. . . .

Jacob went in to his father. . . .

Jacob said . . . , "I am Esau. . . . Eat. . . . Then bless me." . . .

Isaac blessed Jacob. . . .

Three deep lines appeared between Isaac's eyebrows. "Yes, my son. Who are you?" he asked slowly.

"I am Esau, your first son. I have done what you told me. Now sit up and eat some meat of the animal I hunted for you. Then bless me."

Isaac sat up. *Something's wrong here,* he thought to himself. "How did you find and kill the animal so quickly?"

Jacob replied, "Because the Lord your God led me to find it." A cold feeling settled in Jacob's stomach as he told this lie.

Isaac frowned. That voice! There was something about the voice. It sounded more like Jacob's than Esau's.

"Come near so I can touch you, my son. If I can touch you, I will know if you are really my son Esau."[4]

As Jacob knelt over his father's bed, he felt sure Isaac would hear the pounding of his heart. Isaac's thin hand reached out and grasped Jacob's. His fingers explored the back of Jacob's hand, rippling the goat hair that covered it. The scrawny fingers kept exploring, creeping up Jacob's arm. Now the fingers were at his neck.

Haran is famous for its beehive houses. The city has gone by several different names. The Sumerians called it Kaskal, which the Akkadians read as ḥarrânu. The Greeks and Romans knew it as Carrhae.

At last Isaac lay back down. "Your voice sounds like Jacob's voice. But your hands are hairy like the hands of Esau."

Isaac tried to push his doubts away and gather his thoughts so that he might give "Esau" his blessing, but something made him ask once more, "Are you *really* my son Esau?"

Jacob felt that he would strangle, but he answered strongly, "Yes, I am."

At last Isaac ate.

Then, just as Jacob left his father Isaac, Esau came in from hunting. Esau prepared the food in the special way his father enjoyed. Esau brought it to his father. He said, "Father, rise and eat. . . . Then bless me."

Isaac asked, "Who are you?" . . .

"I am . . . Esau." . . .

[Isaac] said, "Then who was it that . . . brought me food before you came? . . . I blessed him." . . .

[Esau] said to his father, "Bless . . . me, too, my father!" . . .

After that Esau hated Jacob. . . .

[Rebekah] said to [Jacob], ". . . Esau is . . . planning to kill you. . . . My brother Laban is living in Haran. Go to him at once!"

When he had finished, he said, "My son, come near and kiss me." Jacob bent to his father and kissed his wrinkled cheek. Isaac breathed deeply of his son's scent. Esau's clothes gave off the wild smell of fields and woods, free of the stench of sheep and goats.

Isaac was satisfied. "The smell of my son is like the smell of the field that the Lord has blessed," he said.

The blessing Isaac uttered sounded like a little poem. "May God give you plenty of rain and good soil. Then you will have plenty of grain and wine. May nations serve you. May peoples bow down to you. May you be master over your brothers. May your mother's sons bow down to you. May everyone who curses you be cursed. And may everyone who blesses you be blessed."[5]

Jacob stumbled from the tent. His heart sang, *I've got it! I've got it! The blessing is mine!* At the same time, the cold feeling in his stomach grew.

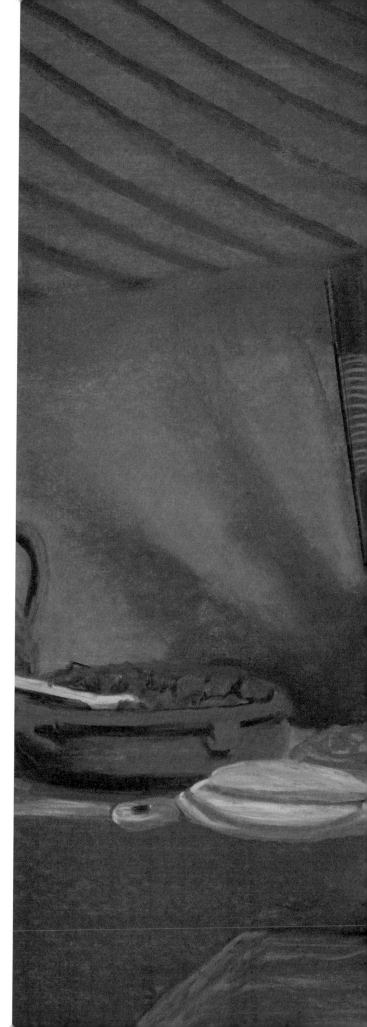

Esau filled a bowl with the meat he had just cooked. Clutching it in both hands, he strode toward his father's tent. Bursting through the tent flap, he called, "Father, rise and eat the food that your son killed for you. Then bless me."

The blood drained from Isaac's face. "Who are you?"

"I am your son—your firstborn son—Esau."

"Then who was it that hunted the animals and brought me food before you came? I ate it, and I blessed him. And it is too late now to take back my blessing."

Esau instantly figured out what had happened. He cried out in anger, "Bless me—me, too, my father!"

Isaac whispered in a hoarse voice, "I can't! Your brother came and tricked me. He has taken your blessing."

Esau flung the bowl and its contents to the

WHAT WERE BLESSINGS AND CURSES?

Did you know there are different kinds of languages? Don't think of German or Tamil. "Kinds of languages" as used here refers to what people mean to accomplish with their words.

Informative language—whether in English or Xhosa!—gives facts. Almanacs consist of informative language. When you read that light travels at 186,000 miles per second, you've read informative language.

If you want to share ideas, you use *cognitive language.* Cognitive language expresses belief and cannot be verified by the senses. "God is love" is cognitive communication. We consider it to be true, but we cannot test God in a laboratory.

Affective language expresses feelings. "Praise be to God!" is affective communication. When a boyfriend tells his girlfriend,

The cornucopia symbolizes bountiful blessing.

"You're the prettiest girl in the whole world," she shouldn't take his words as if they were informative language. He hasn't looked at every female on Planet Earth.

Phatic communication shows friendliness. If you say, "Sure is a nice day!" you are not talking as a meteorologist. You're merely showing that you're not dangerous. When you greet others with "How are you?" you're not really asking for information about their lungs or kidneys or stomach. You're simply being friendly.

Performative language produces an effect. When a sentry calls out "Halt!" you'd better stop. In performative language, words produce an action.

When people in the ancient Near East uttered a curse, which is performative language, they expected that the god would perform what the curse specified. People did not resort to cursing lightly, because the specifics of the curse would follow—or so they expected.

Similarly, blessings were performative language, although people in the ancient Near East didn't know that terminology. People believed that blessings set in motion the stated results. So when Isaac blessed Jacob, saying that Jacob would have much fertile land, everyone expected that Jacob's fields would produce abundant crops.

But surely there was hope. So Esau continued, "Haven't you saved a blessing for me?"

Sorrowfully Isaac answered, "I gave Jacob the power to be master over you. . . . And I kept him strong with grain and wine. There is nothing left to give you, my son."

Esau roared and sobbed. "Do you have only *one* blessing, Father? Bless me, too, Father!"

Isaac's voice, dry and empty as a waterless well, filled the tent as he uttered another poem of blessing—a blessing that sounded more like a curse than a blessing to Esau's ears. "You will live far away from the best land, far from the rain. You will live by using your sword and be a slave to your brother. But when you struggle, you will break free from him."[6]

ground. His eyes flashed with anger. "Jacob is the right name for him," he shouted. "He has tricked me these two times. He took away my share of everything you own. And now he has taken away my blessing."

Esau stormed from the tent. He decided then and there that he would kill Jacob after Isaac died and was buried. And someone overheard him muttering, "I'll kill him! I'll kill him!"

Rebekah heard about Esau's threats and feared

JACOB'S WANDERINGS IN HIS FLIGHT FROM ESAU AND THE MEETING AT THE JABBOK
Starting from Beer-sheba via Bethel, Jacob probably crossed the Jordan, followed the King's Highway to Damascus, Hama (Hamath), Aleppo, and Haran. After 14 years he moved three days' journey from Laban.

for Jacob's life. "Listen," she said to Jacob, "your brother Esau is comforting himself by planning to kill you. So, son, do what I say."

Jacob had already gotten into enough trouble by doing what his mother had told him to do. What did she have in mind now?

"My brother Laban is living in Haran. Go to him at once! Stay with him for a while, until your brother is not so angry. . . . He will forget what you did to him. Then I will send a servant to bring you back."

Rebekah spoke easily, but she felt her heart breaking. Would she ever see Jacob again? She must persuade Isaac to let Jacob go.

"Isaac," she spoke softly as she touched his hand, "I am tired of Hittite women. If Jacob marries one of these Hittite women here in this land, I want to die."[7]

When Isaac said he didn't know what to do about the problem, Rebekah suggested that they send Jacob to Laban's place. There Jacob could find a wife from among her relatives.

Isaac nodded thoughtfully. "Yes," he agreed, "we will send Jacob to the city of Haran."

---

[1]Genesis 27:2, ICB.
[2]Verses 6-9, ICB.
[3]Verses 11-13, ICB.
[4]Verses 18-21, ICB.
[5]Verses 22-29, ICB.
[6]Verses 31-40, ICB.
[7]Verses 42-46, ICB.

Rebekah's Scheme and Jacob's Lie

Isaac was very old and almost blind. "But I can see enough to know that your new wife doesn't worship God," Isaac scolded Esau.

"It doesn't matter," Esau shrugged.

"It matters to God," Isaac said.

One day Isaac became sick. "I must give the birthright blessing to Esau," he said.

Rebekah was upset. Bless Esau? Hadn't the angel said, "The older will serve the younger"?

Isaac called Esau. "Go hunting," Isaac said. "I will eat your meat and bless you."

Rebekah hurried away. "Jacob," she called softly. "We must trick Father. Bring me two goats. I'll cook them. You take the food to Isaac, who will bless you, not Esau."

"I cannot fool Father," Jacob said.

"Yes, you can."

When the goat meat was ready, Rebekah helped Jacob dress in Esau's clothes. She tied goatskins on Jacob's arms and neck. "Now you feel hairy, like Esau."

"Mother . . ."

"Go!"

Jacob entered Isaac's tent. "Here I am, Father," Jacob said in his deepest voice.

"Come near so I can touch you," Isaac said. He touched the hairy goatskins.

"Strange," Isaac said. "You sound like Jacob, but you feel like Esau."

"I am Esau," Jacob lied. Isaac nodded his head. After he had eaten, Isaac said, "Now I will bless you, Esau."

After the blessing, Jacob hurried away. Soon the real Esau came in with his meat.

When Esau discovered Jacob's trick, he got very angry. "That Jacob is a grabber!" he shouted. "He grabbed my birthright, and now he's grabbed my blessing. I will kill him!"

Rebekah was scared. "You must move far away," she told Jacob. "Go live with my relatives."

Jacob slowly nodded his head.

Jacob's lies were now causing big problems.

—Heather Grovet

GOD'S GIFT TO A RUNAWAY

Rebekah shivered when she heard Esau's threats against Jacob's life.

"Jacob," she warned, "your brother Esau is . . . planning to kill you. . . . My brother Laban is living in Haran. Go to him at once! Stay with him for a while, until your brother is not so angry."[1]

Rebekah spoke easily, but she felt her heart breaking. How could she part with this special son who had always helped her and understood her and shared her dreams? The thought *It's all my fault* tormented her.

But she had no time to dwell on that now. She must persuade Isaac to let Jacob go. "Isaac," she spoke softly as she touched his hand, "I am tired of Hittite women. If Jacob marries one of these Hittite women here in this land, I want to die."[2]

Isaac nodded thoughtfully. The greatest sorrow of his life had been Esau's marriages. "Yes," he agreed. "We'll send Jacob to Haran. Ask Jacob to come in."

Hesitantly Jacob entered his father's tent. Shame and guilt slowed his feet as he remembered the last time he stood in this tent and deceived his blind old father. Would his father now turn on him, branding him a cheater and a liar?

"Come close," Isaac invited.

Jacob knelt by his father's bed. Isaac reached out and held Jacob's smooth hand

In ancient times Bethel was called Luz. The modern village of Beitîn, about 12 miles north of Jerusalem, is near the site of the ancient city.

and his father and headed into the hills.

The lengthening shadows of late afternoon kept pace with Jacob's long strides. Normally he would have gloried in the purple shadows and gold-rimmed hills, but now the fear of Esau blinded him to his surroundings. He shrank with terror at the sudden cracking of a twig under his foot or at the harsh squawks of the hoopoe bird.

Esau might even now be stalking him. Never had Jacob felt so alone. He felt he couldn't even ask God to be with him after all he'd done. At last the sun melted behind the gold and purple hills, and a pale moon floated in the sky. The rolling hills, blossoming with white broom plants, glowed eerily in the moonlight. Wearily he sank to the ground, avoiding from long habit the rocks and thistles. Carefully stretching himself along the ground, he lay on his back and gazed into the cold, distant face of the "man in the moon."

between his own. "Go to the house of Bethuel, your mother's father. . . . Laban, your mother's brother, lives there. Marry one of his daughters. May God All-Powerful bless you and give you many children. . . . May the Lord give you and your descendants the blessing of Abraham. Then you may own the land where you are now living as a stranger. This is the land God gave to Abraham."[3]

Jacob stumbled from the tent. Already his mother had gathered a few clothes and a bundle of food for him. Esau, hunting in the desert, would soon return. He must not find Jacob here.

Jacob's lips brushed his mother's cheek. Rebekah clung to him as she whispered, "Shalom!"

Jacob turned his back on his home, his mother,

JACOB'S DREAM

Hours passed. Jacob's body grew cold, his muscles cramped, his eyes felt heavy with weariness, but sleep avoided him. At last Jacob sat up and looked around. In the faint light he could barely make out the outline of a rock just the size and nearly the shape of the

GENESIS 28

Isaac commanded [Jacob], "You must not marry a Canaanite woman. Go to the house of Bethuel, your mother's father. . . . Laban, your mother's brother, lives there. Marry one of his daughters. May God All-Powerful bless you and give you many children. May you become the father of many peoples. May the Lord give you and your descendants the blessing of Abraham. Then you may own the land where you are now living as a stranger." . . .

Jacob left Beersheba and set out for Haran. He came to a place and spent the night there. . . . He found a stone there and laid his head on it to go to sleep. Jacob dreamed that there was a ladder resting on the earth and reaching up into heaven. And he saw angels of God going up and coming down the ladder. And then Jacob saw the

The flying bird is a hoopoe, named after its call: hoo-poo-poo. It is a brazen bird. Its nests are foul-smelling because it doesn't remove the chicks' droppings, as other birds do.

wooden headrest he used for his bed at home.

He reached for the rock and struggled to pull it into place. At last the rock budged, little by little, until Jacob could rest his head upon it and once more stretch his body, full-length, upon the ground. Then, exhausted, he closed his eyes and slept.

Suddenly in his dream a light brighter than the sun bathed the spot in golden splendor. And he saw Lord standing above the ladder. The Lord said, ". . . I will give you and your descendants the land on which you are now sleeping. Your descendants will be as many as the dust of the earth. . . . All the families of the earth will be blessed through you and your descendants. I am with you, and I will protect you everywhere you go. And I will bring you back to this land. I will not leave you until I have done what I have promised you."

Then Jacob woke from his sleep. He said, "Surely the Lord is in this place. But I did not know it." . . . "It is surely the house of God and the gate of heaven."

Jacob rose early in the morning. He took the stone he had slept on and set it up on its end. Then he poured olive oil on the top of it. At first, the name of that city was Luz. But Jacob named it Bethel.

Then Jacob made a promise. . . . "I will give God one-tenth of all he gives me."

before him a golden, gleaming stairway. On its lowest step stood a beautiful, shining being, smiling at him with love and kindness. Behind the beautiful being stood another, then another! Jacob looked up. Angels—hundreds and even thousands of them—moved up and down the shining staircase. Jacob looked up as far as he could see. The stairway stretched on past the highest hills and into the night sky. Alive with the light and movement of heavenly beings, it stretched up past the stars and the darkness beyond. He saw the top of the stairway as it entered heaven. And there stood a Being more beautiful and more dazzling than all the angels. It was God.

"I am . . . the God of Abraham, your grandfather. And I am the God of Isaac. I will give you and your descendants the land on which you are now sleeping. Your descendants will be as many as the dust of the earth. . . . All the families of the earth will be blessed through you and

---

Olive oil was used in many ways in the ancient Near East. It was eaten in foods, burned in lamps, rubbed on the skin, and used in dedicatory rites.

---

your descendants."[4]

Suddenly Jacob found himself sitting bolt upright. The shining staircase and all the shining beings were gone. But God's words rang in his mind and sang in his heart.

God had not left him! God loved him! God had given him a

wonderful gift, a vision filled with angels and love and promises. God loved him just as He loved his grandfather Abraham and would send a whole army of angels to help him.

Jacob thought a lot about the stairway reaching from earth to heaven—God's stairway connecting Him with His children, and he—Jacob—was one of God's children. At the first pink blush of dawn, Jacob reached for his small goatskin bag of olive oil. Solemnly he poured some of the oil over the stone that had cradled his head as he watched the heavenly vision.

"I will call this place Bethel," he said, "because it is a dwelling place of God." Then Jacob continued, saying, "I want God to be with me and to protect me on this journey. . . . If the Lord does these things, he will be my God. This stone which I have set up on its end will be the house of God. And I will give God one-tenth of all he gives me."[5] Jacob picked up his bundle and continued toward Haran. But he no longer jumped with fear at every sound, because he knew that God walked with him.

---

[1]Genesis 27:42-44, ICB.
[2]Verse 46, ICB.
[3]Genesis 28:2-4, ICB.
[4]Verses 13, 14, ICB.
[5]Verses 20-22, ICB.

God's Gift to a Runaway

Jacob stood in his father's tent. He was filled with shame. Jacob had tricked his blind old father. Now Brother Esau wanted to kill him. Would Father be angry too?

But Father Isaac still loved him. "Jacob," he said, "You must go far away and live with Uncle Laban. Marry one of his daughters."

Rebekah and Isaac kissed Jacob good-bye. Rebekah cried as Jacob hurried away, carrying a few clothes and some food. *I must escape before Esau finds me,* Jacob thought. He felt very alone. He trembled with every step. "How can I ask God to help me when I've been so bad?" Jacob wondered.

When it was dark, Jacob finally stopped. He felt very tired, so he lay down on the ground and tried to sleep. He used a stone for a pillow and his extra clothes as a blanket.

Before long Jacob fell asleep.

Suddenly he had a wonderful dream! Jacob saw a beautiful golden staircase going between heaven and earth. Hundreds of shining angels walked up and down the stairs. At the very top of the staircase stood God Himself.

"I am the Lord," God said, "the one true God. I will protect you. I will give you and your children the land on which you are now sleeping. Don't be afraid. You will be a blessing to the entire world."

Jacob was very excited when he woke up. "I will call this place 'Bethel,' because it must be the place where God lives!"

Jacob poured oil on his pillow-stone and prayed. "God, You still love me! If You protect me, Lord, I will worship You forever. And I will give You a tenth of everything I own as an offering to You."

—HEATHER GROVET

JACOB FINDS HIS RELATIVES

The sheep, usually slow-moving, broke into a run as they neared the well. Rachel made a sharp clicking sound with her tongue and raised her arms in a motion the sheep recognized. Immediately they slowed down.

Already, Rachel noticed, three other shepherds had arrived with their flocks. The shepherd boys always stared at her and tumbled over themselves in an effort to get her attention. She never had a difficult time finding someone to move the heavy stone that covered the well.

And she needed help. The stone was so large and heavy that two strong shepherd boys working together strained and struggled as they half lifted, half rolled the well cover to one side.

Out of the corner of her eye Rachel noticed a newcomer to the well. A man, older than the usual shepherd boys, stood talking with them. A snatch of conversation drifted her way. "But look, it is still the middle part of the day. It is not time for the sheep to be gathered for the night. There's still plenty of grazing time."[1]

Obviously the stranger knew something about sheep. Just as surely, he knew nothing about the shepherds' habit in this part of the world of gathering all the flocks together so that they might help each other at the well.

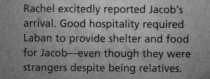

Rachel excitedly reported Jacob's arrival. Good hospitality required Laban to provide shelter and food for Jacob—even though they were strangers despite being relatives.

Rachel's sheep milled around, bleating, impatient for water. Suddenly the stranger ran to the well and with a mighty heave tossed the heavy stone aside. Rachel's eyes grew wide. What strength! But she turned her head aside as she felt the man look at her, his gaze intense.

Then, before she quite knew what was happening, the stranger was watering her sheep. Quickly, with no wasted motions, he filled the watering troughs. Expertly he controlled the greedy sheep, making

GENESIS 29:1-14

[Jacob] came to the land of the people of the East. He looked and saw a well in the field. Three flocks of sheep were lying nearby. . . . A large stone covered the mouth of the well. . . . The shepherds would roll the stone away from the well and water the sheep. Then they would put the stone back in its place.

Jacob said to the shepherds there, "My brothers, where are you from?"

They answered, "We are from Haran."

Then Jacob asked, "Do you know Laban grandson of Nahor?"

They answered, "We know him."

Then Jacob asked, "How is he?"

They answered, "He is well. Look, his daughter Rachel is coming now." . . .

Jacob said, "But look, it is still the middle part of the day. . . . So give [the sheep] water

sure that each sheep drank enough but not too much. Suddenly Rachel felt those same hands on her shoulders and a quick, warm kiss on her cheek. Shocked and confused, she stumbled backward. Who *was* this strange, pushy man? And why did he kiss her?

"Oh, please. . . . I am your relative! I am Jacob, son of Rebekah, your father's sister. I have come all the way from Canaan!"

Rachel looked into Jacob's face. His eyes held a question, an apology, and hope— and something more. For a long moment she gazed into his eyes, unable to look away. Then she smiled that dazzling smile that confused the senses of the local shepherd boys and charmed all who met her.

"Please wait here! I will run and tell my father the news!"

Jacob sank to the ground. His long walk of about 500 miles from his home in the Negev region of southern Canaan to this place near Haran in northern Mesopotamia had left him tired and lonely. But all through the long days and the even longer nights he thought he had felt God's presence. And now God had led him straight to the very well where his uncle's daughter watered her sheep.

⚞⚟

Laban stared at Rachel. *"Rebekah's* son? All the way from Canaan? And all alone? Well, imagine that!"

Laban sprang from his seat on a soft sheepskin and dashed out the door. Down the hill and across the fields he hurried until at last he reached the well outside the city. He paused as he picked out Jacob's lone figure, sitting on top of the well. *Now, why would he come here all alone like this?* Laban asked himself. *Oh, well, time enough to find that out. My sister's son is here!*

Jacob jumped to his feet as he heard Laban's footsteps. Laban threw his arms around him and kissed him on both cheeks. "Welcome, my boy, welcome! Come home with me and tell me all about yourself and your family."

As they walked through Haran's streets, Jacob gazed in wonder. The great city gates, the long, low houses of the rich, the beehive-like houses of the poor, the bustling markets, all reminded him that home was very far away.

Seated comfortably in Laban's home, Jacob answered questions about his family. Yes, his mother was well. His father had been ill when he had left.

Suddenly he found himself pouring out his whole

and let them go back into the pasture."

But they said, "We cannot do that until all the flocks are gathered. Then we will roll away the stone from the mouth of the well and water the sheep."

While Jacob was talking with the shepherds, Rachel came with her father's sheep. . . . Then Jacob saw Laban's daughter Rachel and Laban's sheep. So he went to the well and rolled the stone from its mouth. Then he watered Laban's sheep. . . . Then Jacob kissed Rachel and cried. He told her that he was from her father's family. . . . So Rachel ran home and told her father.

When Laban heard the news about his sister's son Jacob, Laban ran to meet him. Laban hugged him and kissed him and brought him to his house. Jacob told Laban everything that had happened.

Then Laban said, "You are my own flesh and blood."

Jacob and Laban both tended to be devious. Maybe they inherited this trait, as they were related. Marriage between relatives—cousins and even sisters—in the ancient Near East was sought after, so Jacob's marriage to Laban's daughters was desirable.

story into his uncle's listening ear. He told of his longing for the birthright and his father's blessing. He told of Esau's careless attitude. He confessed his guilt in deceiving his blind old father, and he told of Esau's raging anger.

Laban leaned forward as Jacob told of deceiving his father. His eyes looked straight into Jacob's. "And you say Rebekah put you up to this? But you did it, carried out the whole thing, right?"

Jacob squirmed. Behind Laban's polite mask lurked something that made Jacob uneasy. But Laban's voice held no reproof as he urged Jacob to continue.

Finally Jacob told how he had been forced to run away from his own brother and of his fear that he might never see his parents again.

Laban listened carefully, his head forward, eyes half closed but alert behind their heavy lids. When Jacob at last finished his story, Laban murmured, "You *are* my own flesh and blood."[2]

Jacob gave his uncle a sharp look. Did Laban's words mean something more than was on the surface? But Laban's face remained kind and courteous as he once more welcomed Jacob to his home.

---

[1]Genesis 29:7, ICB.
[2]Verse 14, ICB.

Jacob Finds His Relatives

Jacob was dirty and tired. He had walked 500 miles to his mother's country. Now he tried to smile. God had seemed close to him during the long trip, but it was hard to be happy so far from home.

In the distance Jacob saw herds of sheep standing near a well. He walked over to the shepherds. "Do you know a man named Laban?" Jacob asked.

"Yes," the shepherds said. "He lives nearby. This is Laban's daughter Rachel."

A pretty girl smiled shyly at Jacob. Her sheep stood quietly waiting for water.

"Why don't you water the sheep?" Jacob asked, staring at the beautiful girl.

"We have to wait for the others," Rachel said.

"You shouldn't have to wait," Jacob said. He walked over to the well and rolled the heavy stone lid away.

"You are very strong!" Rachel said.

Without thinking, Jacob walked over and kissed Rachel on the cheek. "I'm glad to meet you," he said. "I'm your cousin Jacob."

Rachel rushed home and told her father about the young man at the well.

"He's Rebekah's son?" Laban asked. "Why is he here?"

Laban found Jacob sitting by the well. "Welcome, Jacob!" Laban said. "You must come home with me."

Jacob told Laban and his family everything. "I just wanted to serve God," he said. "But I did everything wrong." He told about Isaac and Rebekah and his twin brother, Esau. "I got Esau's birthright by trading for a bowl of stew, and later I tricked my blind father into giving me the blessing." Laban looked at Jacob carefully. "You are my relative," he said slowly.

Rachel smiled, but said nothing.

Jacob felt better. It was good to be back with family—especially pretty ones like Rachel. Maybe God was with him after all.

—HEATHER GROVET

JACOB'S TURN TO CRY

Jacob made himself useful in his uncle's household. Feeling at home with the flocks, he volunteered to help care for them. In just a matter of weeks all the sheep grew fatter.

Every time he found an opportunity to gaze into Rachel's eyes, Jacob felt he might lose his balance and fall into their dark, sparkling depths. Ever since that first day at the well he had known, somehow, that this girl would change his life. He also remembered his father's parting words, "Marry one of Laban's daughters." But what did he have to offer Laban as a bride price?

"Jacob," Laban began one evening when they had finished supper, "you've been here a month now. You've worked as hard as any of my servants." Laban didn't bother to mention that since Jacob had come, the sheep were fatter, the servants happier, the household more productive, than ever before.

"It is not right for you to keep on working for me without pay. What would you like me to pay you?"[1]

Jacob caught his breath. The very opportunity he had been waiting for had jumped right into his lap! He tried to keep the eagerness from his voice as he answered, "Let me marry your younger daughter Rachel. If you will, I will work seven years for you."[2]

Laban leaned back in his chair, his heavy eyelids veiling his eyes like a curtain, a hand

over his mouth to hide a sudden, secret smile. *Aha!* he thought to himself, *he's offered to work for Rachel, just as I thought he would. But seven years! That's better than I'd hoped for!* Aloud Laban said, "It would be better for her to marry you than someone else. So stay here with me."[3]

Rachel, listening behind the door, felt her heart begin to pound. "Leah! Leah!" she called as she raced into the courtyard where Leah was still cooking food.

In the ancient Near East emotions hardly mattered because marriages were arranged. But with Jacob and Rachel romance played a key role.

Leah turned as her younger sister flew into the courtyard. She felt a quick stab of jealousy as Rachel, with dazzling smile, flashing eyes, and graceful body, did a little dance around the oven. *Why couldn't I look just a little bit like that?* Leah thought regretfully, and not for the first time.

"Oh, Leah," Rachel breathed, "Father has promised me to Jacob. I'm so happy!"

For just an instant a shadow darkened Leah's lovely eyes, but she managed to smile and say, "How nice for you! What kind of agreement did he and Father make?"

Rachel chattered on, telling her sister everything. Instead of giving their father a bride price, Jacob would work seven years for her.

Leah's mind wandered. Seven years. Would anyone want to marry her before seven years had passed? How embarrassing if she should still be single when her younger sister got married! For weeks she had quietly watched Jacob, noting his helpful

GENESIS 29:15-30

Then Laban said to Jacob, ". . . It is not right for you to keep on working for me without pay. What would you like me to pay you?"

Now Laban had two daughters. The older was Leah, and the younger was Rachel. Leah had weak eyes, but Rachel was very beautiful. Jacob loved Rachel. So he said to Laban, "Let me marry your younger daughter Rachel. If you will, I will work seven years for you."

Laban said, "It would be better for her to marry you than someone else. So stay here with me." So Jacob worked for Laban seven years so he could marry Rachel. But they seemed to him like just a few days. . . .

After seven years Jacob said to Laban, "Give me Rachel so that I may marry her. The time I promised to work for you is over."

So Laban gave a feast for all the people

ways and blushing whenever his glance happened to wander in her direction. She had known, of course, that he preferred Rachel.

Under Jacob's care, Laban's flocks grew. Soon Laban had to buy more slaves and hire more servants to care for all his herds. Wisely he made Jacob his manager. Jacob cared for Laban's flocks as if they were his own. At the first sign of a skulking wolf or approaching thief he grabbed his stout shepherd's staff and attacked.

At night, as he rubbed his hands together over a little fire, he often thought of his home and his mother. He wondered if his father still lived, and if Esau was still angry. Painfully, he remembered the day he deceived his blind old father.

Then he'd think of Rachel, and the long, cold nights and the long, hot days passed like the blink of an eye. Months flew by like minutes, and the passing of years—all seven years—seemed only a few days to Jacob, for he loved Rachel so.

THE WEDDING

On a sparkling spring morning when the last of the sheep had been sheared, Jacob approached his uncle. "Uncle," Jacob began, his heart suddenly pounding, "give me Rachel so that I may marry her.

The Syrian wolf, a subspecies of the European wolf, still can be found in areas east of the Jordan River. They were not seen as killing humans but as killers of livestock.

The time I promised to work for you is over."[4]

"Ah, yes," Laban replied. It seemed that Jacob would not be put off any longer. His nephew wanted to marry Rachel, then head back to Canaan. But he, Laban, would think of a way to keep the best shepherd he'd ever had and smartest manager he'd ever seen right here with him. "Well, of course, my boy," he purred. "Leave everything to me."

Laban's household busily prepared for the week-long wedding feast. Tasty sweets and breads and fruits and cheeses were everywhere. Leah and her father had worked so hard on the plans for the wedding that Rachel had nothing at all to worry about.

Only three more days! Jacob told himself, a glad

there. That evening Laban brought his daughter Leah to Jacob. Jacob and Leah [got married]. . . . (Laban gave his slave girl Zilpah to his daughter to be her servant.) In the morning Jacob saw that he had [gotten married to] Leah! He said to Laban, "What have you done to me? I worked hard for you so that

I could marry Rachel! Why did you trick me?"

Laban said, "In our country we do not allow the younger daughter to marry before the older daughter. But complete the full week of the marriage ceremony with Leah. I will give you Rachel to marry also. But you must serve me another seven years."

So Jacob did this, and completed the week with Leah. Then Laban gave him his daughter Rachel as a wife. (Laban gave his slave girl Bilhah to his daughter Rachel to be her servant.) So Jacob [married] Rachel also. And Jacob loved Rachel more than Leah. Jacob worked for Laban for another seven years.

WHAT WAS THE MATTER WITH LEAH?

smile playing about his mouth. Unlike most couples marrying at that time, Jacob and Rachel would marry for love—not for convenience.

Then, when her marriage was so close she could almost feel Jacob's arms around her, Rachel listened in shock and disbelief as her father spoke. "You cannot marry before your sister does. Leah must marry first. Therefore, Leah, not you, will become Jacob's bride."

"Father!" Rachel pleaded. "Jacob will never agree!"

"Jacob will never know until it is too late. The night hides many things, and it will hide your sister from him. The heavy wedding veil will cover Leah's face, and like a proper, shy bride, she will remain silent on her wedding day."

"No, no, no!"

Leah had weak eyes, but Rachel was very beautiful" (Genesis 29:17, ICB).

Sometimes the way we ask a question predetermines the answer. "What was the matter with Leah?" presupposes a negative answer. We assume that she had a problem—with her eyes. Was she nearsighted? Farsighted? Cross-eyed? Walleyed? Might the color of her eyes have been unattractive?

Some translations of Genesis 29:17 imply that Leah had defective eyes. This is in contrast with Rachel, who is spoken of in glowing terms. But maybe we need to reframe the question. Maybe we need to ask: What was right with Leah? What was her asset? It is possible that both parts of verse 19 refer to a beautiful feature of each sister.

The Hebrew adjective translated "weak" in the ICB is *rak*. It is used fewer than 20 times in the Bible, and usually it does not have negative overtones. Notice the italicized word in the following examples. "A *soft* answer turneth away wrath: but grievous words stir up anger" (Proverbs 15:1, KJV). "And Abraham ran unto the herd, and fetched a calf *tender* and good, and gave it

Jacob didn't find Leah's doe-like eyes nearly as exciting as Rachel's figure.

unto a young man; and he hasted to dress it" (Genesis 18:7, KJV). "And David said, Solomon my son is young and *tender*" (1 Chronicles 22:5, KJV).

So, what about Leah? A growing number of biblical scholars now think that Genesis 29:17 gives the physical assets of both girls, though Rachel clearly has the edge in Jacob's eyes! Leah, thus, has lovely eyes. Dainty. Very feminine! Indeed, several versions of Scripture give a positive value to Leah's eyes. "Leah had lovely eyes" (TEV). Jewish scholar S. R. Hirsch in his translation of the Pentateuch points out that the verse actually praises Leah's good point.

In 1966 the *Jerusalem Bible* translated the verse "There was no sparkle in Leah's eyes." But the 1985 *New Jerusalem Bible* reads: "Leah had lovely eyes." Similarly, the Revised Standard Version in 1971 rendered the passage: "Leah's eyes were weak." The New Revised Standard Version of 1989 says: "Leah's eyes were lovely."

And what about Rachel's assets? The Hebrew wording indicates that she had a knockout figure, and Jacob loved her (Genesis 29:18)!

© DIGITAL VISION

Rachel moaned. "How can you do this to him?"

"I have a feeling," Laban mused, "that Jacob may understand better than you think."

"Well, *I* don't understand, and I won't let you and Leah do this to us!"

"My daughter," Laban's voice was chill, "you forget yourself. You will honor and obey me. If you have any foolish notions of telling Jacob about this, forget them. He might just leave for Canaan immediately, and then what would you have accomplished?

Perhaps Jacob had indulged in too many refreshments at his wedding. Maybe the room was too dark. Regardless, he was traumatized when he woke up the next morning married to Leah, not Rachel.

have you done to me? What have you done? Where is my Rachel? I've married *Leah!* Laban! Where are you, Laban?" Then his voice fell to a broken whisper: "Rachel! Rachel!"

Rachel groaned as she heard Jacob's words and felt his suffering. Then she heard her father's voice.

"There you are!" Jacob stormed. "You tricked me!" But as he said the words, a look of pained understanding crossed his face. Was this what it felt like to be deceived? Jacob covered his face with his hands and listened to Laban's smooth words. "In our country we do not allow the younger daughter to marry before the older daughter. But complete the full week of the marriage ceremony with Leah. I will give you Rachel to marry also. But you must serve me another seven years."[5]

Jacob looked into Laban's eyes and saw his own reflection captured there. *Trapped!* he thought. *Laban has trapped me!* But still devoted to Rachel, Jacob replied with bitter tone, "I'll do it."

Go along with this quietly, and at the end of their marriage week I will arrange for you to marry him also."

The sounds of merriment began. Rachel heard the babble and laughter of many voices. Family and friends celebrated with Laban as he offered his hospitality to the wedding guests. She pictured Jacob, happy, glowing, as he looked at his bride, lavishly dressed and veiled, a crown upon her head. *Rachel,* he would be thinking, *Rachel!* But with the dawn of day he would know; he would see—Leah!

The dawn's pale light found Rachel dry-eyed but trembling with exhaustion. *Jacob, oh, Jacob,* she moaned softly to herself, *I don't think I'll ever forgive Father for this!*

Then a cry, dreadful in its anguish, pierced the still air, and Jacob staggered into the light. "What

[1]Genesis 29:15, ICB.
[2]Verse 18, ICB.
[3]Verse 19, ICB.
[4]Verse 21, ICB.
[5]Verses 26, 27, ICB.

Jacob's Turn to Cry

Jacob worked hard caring for Uncle Laban's sheep. Soon the sheep were fat and healthy.

"You are a good worker," Laban told Jacob one evening. "I need to pay you. What would you like for pay?"

Jacob blushed. *I love Rachel,* he thought, *and she loves me.*

"Uncle," Jacob said slowly, "I will work for you for seven years if you will allow me to marry Rachel."

"Rachel?" Laban asked. He thought for a moment. "Yes, that would be fine," he agreed.

Rachel was excited when she heard that Jacob wanted to marry her. But Rachel's older sister, Leah, wasn't so happy.

I love Jacob too, Leah thought. *But Jacob doesn't love me.*

Jacob loved Rachel so much that the seven years seemed to pass in a few days. Finally it was time for the wedding.

"This is the happiest day of my life!" Jacob said.

But Jacob's happiness soon came to an end. Uncle Laban tricked him!

When Jacob woke up the morning after the wedding, it wasn't Rachel sleeping beside him. It was Leah!

"Father made me obey him," Leah sobbed. "He knew you would never recognize me under my heavy wedding clothes. He said you'd learn to love me."

"But I don't love you!" Jacob yelled. "I love Rachel!"

Leah sobbed louder.

Jacob rushed to find Uncle Laban. "What have you done?" Jacob hollered.

Laban spoke sly words. "I could never let the younger girl get married first. Don't worry. If you work for another seven years, I'll let you marry Rachel, too."

"You lied!" Jacob yelled. Then Jacob stopped. Many years earlier he had tricked his father and brother. Now someone had tricked him.

But Jacob still loved Rachel. "I'll do it," he said angrily. "I'll work another seven years for the woman I love."

—HEATHER GROVET

ONCE MORE A RUNAWAY

For the hundredth time Jacob glanced fearfully over his shoulder. At any moment Laban and a troop of armed servants might descend upon him and his runaway household.

Jacob smiled a bitter little smile at the thought. He had arrived in Haran as a runaway *to* Laban. Now he was a runaway again—this time *from* Laban. Rachel, riding beside him, gave him a reassuring smile.

At least I have Rachel with me, thought Jacob. *But I never dreamed when I left Canaan that it would be 20 years before I headed home again!*

Jacob's hundreds of cows and sheep and goats plodded on. From the backs of camels, Jacob's wives and their children slowly lurched toward Canaan. Other servants and Jacob's older sons herded the flocks while the younger children scampered about, sometimes running ahead of the flocks, sometimes tagging along behind.

Laban had been away to shear his sheep when Jacob left, but after several days Laban had discovered Jacob's disappearance, gathered his men together, and given chase.

But God had not forgotten Jacob. One starry night in Haran he had dreamed of the home he had left, and God had spoken to him. "I am the God who appeared to you at Bethel. . . . Now I want you to leave here. Go back to the land where you were born."[1]

As Jacob had listened to that voice, he knew that the long, weary, homesick years were at an end.

Now as the sun trailed its fiery fingers across the evening sky, Jacob knew they must stop and make camp for the night. Perhaps if they left very early in the morning, Laban might not catch up with them.

Next morning in the early light Jacob moved quietly from tent to tent. "Let's go," he spoke softly, urgently. "Gather the flocks together. Don't build any fires to cook your food. We'll eat as we go. Hurry!"

But his words were suddenly swallowed up in a great clatter of loud voices mingled with the brays of donkeys and the clank of swords. Then Laban, his squat figure looming larger than life in the dim morning light, leaped from his mount and stood before Jacob. It had taken him seven days to catch up with Jacob.

Jacob and his family had crossed the Euphrates River, which was about 50 miles from Laban's place, and continued their flight westward.

"Jacob, my son," he purred in the phony way that Jacob knew so well, "what have you done? . . . Why did you trick me? Why didn't you tell me? Then I could send you away with joy and singing."

GENESIS 31:1-21

One day Jacob heard Laban's sons talking. They said, "Jacob has taken everything our father owned. Jacob has become rich in this way." Then Jacob noticed that Laban was not as friendly as he had been before. The Lord said to Jacob, "Go back to the land where your ancestors lived. I will be with you."

So Jacob told Rachel and Leah to meet him in the field where he kept his flocks. He said to them, "I have seen that your father is not as friendly with me as he used to be. But the God of my father has been with me. You both know that I have worked as hard as I could for your father. But he cheated me. He has changed my pay ten times. But God has not allowed your father to harm me." . . .

Rachel and Leah answered Jacob, "Our father has nothing to give us when he dies. He has treated us like strangers. He sold us

Laban paused for effect. "You did not even let me kiss my grandchildren and my daughters goodbye," he finished with a catch in his voice.

Jacob regarded his uncle with disgust. What a performance!

Now Laban's voice took on a more threatening tone. "You were very foolish to do this! I have the power to harm you." Laban continued his scolding, "But"—and for an instant Laban's face shone with sincerity—"last night the God of your father spoke to me. He warned me not to say anything to you, good or bad."

Jacob caught his breath. How wonderfully his God watched over him!

"I know you want to go back to your home. But why did you steal my idols?"

This new accusation stunned Jacob, and he didn't know what to say. Steal Laban's idols? He would never do that!

But Laban thought, *He's done me one better this time! He's stolen my gods.*

Jacob stalled. "I left without telling you, because I was afraid!" he mumbled. Then, with a return of confidence, he firmly stated, "If you find anyone here who has taken your idols, he will be killed!"[2]

Rachel, listening from her tent, felt the color

Music played an important role in the ancient world. String, wind, and percussion instruments were common. The reliefs of these musicians come from Ur and date to about 2600 B.C.

drain from her face. Her eyes darted to a pile of blankets where she had hidden the household gods. She had told no one about the gods. Not even Jacob knew she'd taken them.

Now Laban roared to his servants, "Search the tents. Leave nothing unturned! We will find those idols before we leave here!"

Rachel peeked out of her tent. Ah! The search had begun in a tent far from hers. She had time—just a little time!

Laban and his servants stormed through the camp. They tore into neatly stacked blankets, bags of cooking pots, baskets of grain. They tossed clothing

"SEARCH THE TENTS. LEAVE NOTHING UNTURNED! WE WILL FIND THOSE IDOLS BEFORE WE LEAVE HERE!"

to you, and then he spent all of the money you paid for us. God took all this wealth from our father, and now it belongs to us and our children. So you do whatever God told you to do."

So Jacob put his children and his wives on camels. Then they began their journey back to Isaac, his father. He lived in the land of Canaan. All the flocks of animals that Jacob owned walked ahead of them. He carried everything with him that he had gotten while he lived in Northwest Mesopotamia.

Laban was gone to cut the wool from his sheep. While he was gone, Rachel stole the idols of false gods that belonged to him. And Jacob tricked Laban the Aramean. He did not tell Laban he was leaving. Jacob and his family left quickly. They crossed the Euphrates River and traveled toward the mountains of Gilead.

Whether angry or content, well-mannered ancient Near Easterners tried to work out arrangements whereby both parties' honor could be maintained. This involved what we would consider haggling.

around and knocked the pins out from under the tents. Jacob followed, his face grim.

Finally Laban barged into Rachel's tent, where she sat quietly with her skirt draped over her camel's saddle basket. She did not rise as her father entered, but he was so intent on his search he hardly glanced at her. Again he rummaged through blankets and clothes and peeked into every little corner and

cranny of the tent. At last he straightened and glared at Rachel.

Rachel smiled sweetly. "Father, don't be angry with me, but I am not able to stand up before you. I am not feeling good."

Laban stormed from the tent, baffled. He'd searched everywhere! Rachel slowly let out a shaky breath and shifted her position. She would have to

TERAPHIM

sit on the little house-hold idols a while longer, until she was sure her father had left the campsite!

Suddenly Jacob's pent-up anger exploded. "What law have I broken to cause you to chase me? You have looked through everything I own. But you have found nothing that belongs to you. If you have found anything, show it to everyone." Jacob gave a short little laugh.

"I have worked for you now for 20 years. During all that time none of the lambs and kids died during birth. And I have not eaten any of the male sheep from your flocks. . . . I worked like a slave for you for 20 years. For the first 14 years I worked to get your two daughters. The last 6 years I worked to earn your animals. And during that time you changed my pay ten times."[3] Jacob's face was white with anger, and his dark eyes blazed as he remembered the misery of the past 20 years.

Laban's half-closed eyes revealed nothing. He raised a hand as if to quiet Jacob, but Jacob had more to say.

Laban challenges Jacob, "Why did you steal my idols?" The Hebrew word for idols is teraphim. Not all scholars agree on the root meaning of the word, but many think the word means something like "lifeless things" or "decaying things" or "perishing things."

Today at nearly every archaeological site in Bible lands little figurines are unearthed—probably what Scripture here refers to as teraphim. These figurines are made from clay, wood, and even costly metals. Most of them are about two to three inches tall, though elsewhere in the Bible they are described in such a way that at least some of them must have been life-size. The vast majority are of naked females with exaggerated sexual features, though a few are of males.

Why would Rachel steal her father's gods? Teraphim seem to have served various functions. Sometimes they were consulted for advice—used in a kind of divination, something like modern crystal balls. There is some evidence from documents found at Nuzi (in ancient Mesopotamia, the same general area where Laban lived) that whoever owned the family gods would also inherit the estate upon the patriarch's death. There is also the distinct possibility that women wore them as amulets or worshipped them in an attempt to be fertile. (Having children was especially important in the ancient Near East, and childless women were considered as being cursed.)

One can understand, then, that Rachel might have had a number of reasons for stealing her father's idols. She may have thought that she would then be able to inherit the estate if she owned them. She may have thought they would bring her good luck or even paranormal guidance. She may have assumed that they would afford her protection on the long trek from Mesopotamia to Canaan. And since she had not given birth to children, she may have hoped they'd make her fertile. (She later ate mandrake roots, which were supposed to be an aphrodisiac and/or fertility drug. See Genesis 30:14-16.)

Assuming that Rachel was telling the truth about her condition, the irony in this particular account is that gods were to be kept pure, undefiled, yet she was sitting "on" them during her monthly period, which would have defiled the teraphim, making them "unclean." (The Mosaic law declared menstruating women unclean during their monthly periods.)

In Genesis 35:2-4 we read that Jacob made his household throw away their idols before they headed for Bethel, where they settled.

"But the God of my father was with me. . . . If God had not been with me, you would have sent me away with nothing. But he saw the trouble I had and the hard work I did. And last night God corrected *you*."

Laban studied Jacob's face. He could easily see

that Jacob was angry, very angry. Suppose Jacob hooked up with his brother Esau, a mighty warrior, and came back to attack him? *I'd better see what I can do to smooth this over,* he thought. *But I won't admit doing anything wrong!*

"Jacob," he began, his tone friendly, "these girls are my daughters. Their children belong to me, and these animals are mine. Everything you see here belongs to me."

Jacob felt the hot blood rush to his temples, but Laban hurried on. "I can do nothing to keep my daughters and their children. Let us make an agreement."[4]

Jacob wasn't fooled by Laban's words. *He's afraid that I'll come back and attack him, because that's what*

he'd do to me! Jacob thought. But he agreed.

Laban and Jacob quickly gathered a pile of rocks. As they worked together, picking up the stones and wedging them on top of each other, Jacob looked at Laban. Could there be friendship between them? Would Laban at last confess his wrongs to Jacob and ask forgiveness? But Laban's eyes, beneath their sleepy lids, were as cold and hard as the stones he handled.

At last Laban spoke up. "Let the Lord watch over us while we are separated from each other. . . . I will never go past this pile to hurt you. And you must never come to my side of them to hurt me. . . . Let God punish either of us if we break this agreement."[5]

Jacob permitted himself a little smile, but he solemnly promised. Then they offered a sacrifice to God and prepared a big meal for everyone to eat. The next morning Laban strolled through the camp, stopping to kiss his grandchildren goodbye and saying farewell to his daughters.

Then, with a quick leap to the back of a donkey, he rode away, his squat form getting smaller and smaller in the distance, finally disappearing in a cloud of dust.

The origin of kissing remains unknown. The kiss was an affable gesture when greeting or leave-taking relatives and friends. It was not generally regarded as erotic.

[1]Genesis 31:13, ICB.
[2]Verses 26-32, ICB.
[3]Verses 35-41, ICB.
[4]Verses 42-44, ICB.
[5]Verses 48-52, ICB.

Once More a Runaway

"Rachel, Leah," Jacob called softly. "Come here." Jacob looked around carefully before speaking. "I have lived here 20 years, but your father acts as if I am his enemy. Last night God told me to return to my old country."

"That's good," Rachel said. "Father has treated you badly."

"Yes," Leah agreed. "He's even unkind to us—his own daughters."

"We must sneak away," Jacob said. "Otherwise Laban will stop us."

"Sneak?" Rachel asked. "How? You have many children, animals, and servants."

"We will leave when your father is away," Jacob said. "Go. Pack for our big trip."

Soon Jacob and his family began their long walk back to Jacob's old country. On the seventh day Laban and his soldiers caught up to Jacob.

"Stop!" Laban shouted. "Thieves! You left without asking for my permission."

"I have taken nothing that belongs to you," Jacob said. "I have worked hard for everything that you see here."

"Ha!" Laban yelled. "You lie! Someone stole my idols!"

"Never!" Jacob said. "But search our things. If you find any of your gods, you may kill the person who took them."

Rachel turned pale. Jacob didn't know she had taken the idols from Laban's house!

Quickly Rachel ran to her tent and hid the idols under a camel saddle. Then she sat on the saddle.

When Laban and the soldiers entered Rachel's tent, she didn't get up. And Laban didn't find the idols.

Jacob and Laban decided to make peace with each other. They built a stone wall, and each man agreed to stay on their own side of the wall. Then Laban rode away, allowing Jacob and his family to continue on their trip to the land of Canaan.

—HEATHER GROVET

NIGHT OF SILENT COMBAT

Getting closer to Esau! Getting closer to Esau! The words beat a rhythm in Jacob's head with each step he took. His heart pounded with the old fear as he remembered Esau's words: "I'll kill him if it's the last thing I ever do!"

Had Esau heard that Jacob was returning to Canaan? He could imagine Esau's reaction. He'd probably round up his friends and relatives from the fierce tribes of the Ishmaelites and the Hittites and attack Jacob's caravan!

There's no way I can protect my wives and children and servants from an army like that! Jacob mused to himself.

God understood that Jacob was frightened, and just for an instant He opened Jacob's eyes to see a beautiful sight. A company of angels hovered over his camp, protecting it, guarding it. Every lamb, every servant, every child moved within the shadow of an angel's wings.

Jacob stood with shining eyes and fast-beating heart as he looked at God's messengers. Memories overwhelmed him. He remembered, as a child, looking at clouds and "seeing" angels. The vision God had given him of the shining staircase with angels gliding up and down its sparkling steps flashed through his mind.

"There are two camps here!" Jacob exclaimed. "Mine and God's! This is the camp of

God." So Jacob called this place Mahanaim, which in Hebrew meant "two camps."

Then he turned to his servants. "Ebal! Adoniram! This is what I want you to do. Go find my brother Esau in the country of Edom. Tell him that I, Jacob, his brother, have lived with Laban and have remained there until now. I have cattle, donkeys, flocks, and male and female servants. I send this message to you and ask that you accept us."

Jacob waited anxiously for the return of the messengers, but the word they brought gave him no comfort. "We went to your brother Esau. He is

Because there were no bridges, rivers had to be crossed at places where they were relatively shallow. It is difficult to find good fording spots in the spring, when the rivers swell from snowmelt.

GENESIS 32:22-31

During the night Jacob rose and crossed the Jabbok River at the crossing. He took his 2 wives, his 2 slave girls and his 11 sons with him. He sent his family and everything he had across the river. But Jacob stayed behind alone. And a man came and wrestled with him until the sun came up. The man saw that he could not defeat Jacob. So he struck Jacob's hip and put it out of joint.

Then the man said to Jacob, "Let me go. The sun is coming up."

But Jacob said, "I will let you go if you will bless me."

The man said to him, "What is your name?"

coming to meet you. And he has 400 men with him."[1]

No message, no words of reassurance or forgiveness, thought Jacob. *I'd better prepare for the worst.*

Quickly Jacob divided his caravan into two groups. As Jacob directed, men and women and boys and girls grabbed their belongings and hurried to join one of the two groups. *Now,* Jacob thought, *if Esau attacks one group, perhaps the other can escape!*

Then Jacob prayed harder than he had ever prayed before. "God of my father Abraham! God my father Isaac! Lord, you told me to return to my country and my family. You said that you would do good to me. I am not worthy of the kindness and continual goodness you have shown me. . . . Please save me from my brother Esau. I am afraid he will come and kill all of us, even the mothers with the children."[2]

Jacob reminded God of His promise, "I will do good to you. I will make your children as many as the sand of the seashore."[3]

Early the next morning Jacob hurried through the camp, barking orders.

"Seth, cut out 200 of my best nanny goats from the herd, and 20 of the billy goats!

"You, Amos! Round up 200 ewes and 20 rams. Keep them separate from Seth's flock!

"Zippor! Put 30 milking camels with their calves in a herd with 40 cows, 10 bulls, 20 female donkeys, and 10 males. Hurry, but don't frighten the animals! I want them to be in good shape when they reach Esau!"

"What are you doing, Father?" 12-year-old Reuben asked in wonder.

"I'm sending your uncle Esau some presents, hoping to soften his heart before we meet him! My servants will give him one flock after another. They'll tell him that I, his servant, send them to him, my master. Pray, Reuben, that these gifts will persuade my brother to forgive me for a wrong I did him years ago!"

As night fell, Jacob and his caravan found themselves at the fording place of the Jabbok, a clear mountain stream. The shadows of night turned the waters black as they gurgled and sparkled under a pale moon. Jacob thought quickly. They must cross the Jabbok. Should they do it now, in the darkness, or wait for tomorrow, when Esau's troops might catch them in the middle of the stream? He decided—they must cross tonight!

Carefully guarding each animal, Jacob and his servants guided the flocks as they splashed through the stream. Sure-footed donkeys, their backs piled high with blankets, tents, pots, and pans, marched sedately across the stream, stopping now and then to drink from the dark water.

> "PLEASE SAVE ME FROM MY BROTHER ESAU. I AM AFRAID HE WILL COME AND KILL ALL OF US, EVEN THE MOTHERS WITH THE CHILDREN."

And he answered, "Jacob."

Then the man said, "Your name will no longer be Jacob. Your name will now be Israel, because you have wrestled with God and with men. And you have won."

Then Jacob asked him, "Please tell me your name."

But the man said, "Why do you ask my name?" Then he blessed Jacob there.

So Jacob named that place Peniel. He said, "I have seen God face to face. But my life was saved." Then the sun rose as he was leaving that place. Jacob was limping because of his leg.

At last the women and children crossed. Some rode on camels or donkeys. The older children waded bravely into the water, grinning at each other as they felt the water rising. "I'm not afraid!" they told one another. But they kept close to a donkey's tail or a mother's long skirt, just in case they needed something to grab if a stone rolled under their feet or a surge of water buckled their knees.

JACOB'S WRESTLING MATCH

Jacob, astride a donkey, rode endlessly back and forth, back and forth, checking to see that no one got left behind. He especially checked the baby animals, making sure that none had tired of swimming and been swept downstream. He checked and double-checked to see that all the servants and his wives and children had at last reached the other side of the Jabbok.

Finally Jacob dismounted and stood on the north bank, his household safely across on the other side. Darkness had now fallen.

Suddenly he felt a heavy hand on his shoulder. *Esau!* he thought. Jacob wheeled and grabbed the stranger's arms, pinning them behind his back. Silently, quickly, easily, the stranger broke Jacob's hold and gripped him in one of his own. With all his strength Jacob bent the stranger backward until he released his hold on him.

Jacob's heart pounded and he gasped for breath, but the stranger breathed easily. Jacob tried to see in the thin moonlight who this person was. *This isn't Esau!* Jacob thought. *I don't know who it is, but he's not hairy like Esau!*

Hour after hour Jacob struggled with the stranger. The night seemed a hundred years long. The moon hid itself behind a cloud and refused to show its face again. Jacob panted. Cold sweat trickled down his body, but the stranger seemed as fresh as when he had first laid his hand on Jacob's shoulder.

I can't go on with this much longer! Jacob thought. *Why doesn't he just kill me and get it over with? I know he can do it, and so does he!* But the struggle went on and on. As Jacob lifted an arm, heavy with exhaustion, or twined his leg around the stranger's, the thought came to him, *This person cannot be human!*

Finally the first pale light of dawn edged the eastern sky. At that moment the stranger lifted one finger and touched Jacob's hip. Pain, grinding pain, shot through his joint, and he fell to the earth, moaning. Still Jacob kept his arms wrapped tightly around the stranger's legs. The thought struck Jacob with terrible force: *I must be wrestling with an angel, or maybe with God Himself!*

Then, for the first time, the stranger spoke.

The Jabbok River still exists and is known as *Nahr ez-Zerqā*, which means "Blue River." It flows into the Jordan River about 25 miles north of the Dead Sea.

"Let me go. The sun is coming up."

"I will let you go if you will bless me," Jacob cried, desperate for a blessing, and full of wonder that he held God, in the form of a man, right in his arms.

"What is your name?" the stranger asked gently, a smile in his voice.

"Jacob."

"Your name will no longer be Jacob. Your name will now be Israel, because you have wrestled with God and with men. And you have won."

Jacob knew he had not won the fight, but he had never given up. "Please tell me your name," Jacob whispered.

The stranger answered, "Why do you ask my name?" Then He blessed Jacob, for the Stranger was none other than God Himself.

The next morning Jacob limped into camp, his face radiant. Everyone stared at him, wondering where the fear had gone, wondering where his worry went, wondering why he grabbed his hip in pain but smiled such a beautiful smile.

"I have seen God face to face. But my life was saved," he shouted.[4] "Why should I worry about meeting Esau?"

Brand has chosen to give names to Jacob's servants—Ebal, Adoniram, Seth, Amos, Zippor. These are good Hebrew names, but in the Bible they refer to people of a different time and place. By giving names to the servants, Brand is adding what we would call verisimilitude to the story, making it come alive.

[1]Genesis 32:6, ICB.
[2]Verses 9-11, ICB.
[3]Verse 12, ICB.
[4]Verses 26-30, ICB.

Night of Silent Combat

Jacob was very worried as his family continued their long walk to his home country. *Esau said he'd kill me!* Jacob thought. *Suppose he learns that I'm going back home? How can I protect my family?*

Jacob called his servants. "Run ahead and tell Esau we are coming as friends," he said.

When the servants returned, they brought back bad news. "Esau is coming with 400 men!"

"An army!" Jacob groaned. "Esau wants to kill me and maybe even my wives and children!"

Jacob prayed harder than ever. God spoke to Jacob. "Be brave. I will care for you."

In the morning Jacob called his servants again. "I am going to send presents to Esau. We need many sheep, goats, cows, and donkeys."

Jacob sent these gifts ahead for Esau.

Late that night Jacob's family crossed the cold river Jordan. The family fell into an exhausted sleep—everyone except Jacob.

Jacob stood in the dark, worrying, when someone grabbed him from behind.

Esau! Jacob thought wildly. Jacob struggled with the dark stranger, pushing and fighting back. Hour after hour Jacob struggled with the powerful stranger. *This isn't Esau,* Jacob thought. *But who is it? Maybe I'm fighting with an angel, or even with God!*

Finally the man touched Jacob's hip. Jacob screamed in pain. "I can't move my hip, but I won't let you go until you bless me," Jacob cried.

"Who are you?" the stranger asked.

"Jacob."

"I give you a new name," the man said. "Now you will be called Israel, meaning 'Someone who has power with God.'" Then the Stranger blessed Jacob, for the Stranger was God Himself!

With a big smile on his face, Jacob limped back to his family. "I have lived to see God," he said. "Why should I worry about meeting Esau?"

—HEATHER GROVET

FORGIVEN AND TWICE BLESSED!

Donkeys brayed, cows bellowed, and sheep and goats bleated as the warm morning sunshine roused them to start another day. Even though 97-year-old Jacob was limping after his wrestling match with God, he felt more energetic and enthusiastic than he had in years.

"Everyone get ready. Now!" he ordered. "Somehow I feel that this is the day I will see my brother, Esau!" he told no one in particular. "Maybe he should meet the servants first with their children—just in case . . ."

Wives, concubines, children, and servants scurried to their places in the group. At the front of the large crowd stood Bilhah and Zilpah, special servants for Rachel and Leah, with their noisy children laughing and playing.

At the very back of the group, Rachel sat on a donkey. At her side a smaller donkey pranced while little Joseph straddled it, his feet sticking straight out from its sides like tiny wings. Joseph's hands, small and brown, clutched the bridle. Suddenly he pulled on it with all his strength. "Whoa!" he shouted to the donkey. Rachel laughed, a warm and tender sound.

"I'll be at the front to meet Esau," Jacob told them. "But I'll be back!"

As Jacob limped to the front of the group, a thousand thoughts tried to fit in his mind

at one time. Words exploded in his head: *Deception. Angels. Bethel. I'll kill him! Israel.*

JACOB MEETS ESAU

Like a mighty army Esau and his men spread in front of Jacob's group—400 men who looked like soldiers! Esau, himself bigger and shaggier, his wild red beard flecked with gray, looked very scary. His dark eyes met Jacob's.

For an instant Jacob returned the look, then he bowed low before Esau. He stood up, and bowed again—and again! Seven times Jacob bowed to Esau, showing him the respect due a king. Every bow said, I'm not here to trick you again, Esau; I'm here to apologize! Meanwhile Jacob's family and flocks began to appear around the bend. It took a long time for such a large group to come into view.

Suddenly Esau dashed forward. Jacob froze in his tracks. But then he saw tears streaming down Esau's face. The two long-separated brothers threw their arms around each other and kissed each other and cried. God had heard Jacob's prayer.

Esau cleared his throat and looked at all the people in Jacob's caravan. "Who are these people with you?"[1] he asked. "When you left home you had no one!"

Jacob smiled at his children. "These are the children God has given me," he said proudly. "God has been good to me, your servant."[2] Jacob introduced everyone to Esau. Everyone bowed to Esau, but little Joseph couldn't help peeking up at the great hairy man as he did so.

"Now, Jacob," Esau asked in a softer tone, "I saw many herds as I was coming here. Why did you bring them?"[3] Esau knew exactly what Jacob intended, but he wanted to hear the words from Jacob himself.

"They were to please you, my master."[4]

Esau smiled. "I already have enough, my brother. Keep what you have."[5]

Jacob grew very serious. "No! Please! If I have pleased you, then please accept the gift I give you. I am very happy to see your face again. It is like seeing the face of God because you have accepted me."[6]

"I really couldn't take them!" Esau countered.

"I beg you to accept the gift I give you."[7]

"Very well, then, if you insist!" Esau agreed.

"Wonderful! Wonderful!" And Jacob felt a burden lifted. God had forgiven him long ago for his sin. Now his brother had forgiven him. Could he at last forgive himself?

The twins had a lot of catching up to do. Jacob was full of questions, but he spoke carefully, afraid of the answers. He cleared his throat. "About our father," he began. "I suppose he died many years ago?"

Esau smiled. "No! You'd be surprised. He recovered from his illness and has learned to get along very well, even though blind. In fact, he's still very much in charge of things, dealing with the servants and overseeing the flocks."

"That's wonderful!" Jacob exclaimed. "I've missed him so." Now eager to ask his next question, Jacob said, "And Mother. How is Mother?"

Esau quickly looked away. "Mother died several years ago," he said simply.

GENESIS 33:1-17

Jacob looked up and saw Esau coming. With him were 400 men. . . . [Jacob] bowed down flat on the ground seven times as he was walking toward his brother.

But Esau ran to meet Jacob. Esau put his arms around him and hugged him. Then Esau kissed him, and they both cried. . . .

Esau said, "I saw many herds as I was coming here. Why did you bring them?"

Jacob answered, "They were to please you, my master."

But Esau said, "I already have enough, my brother. Keep what you have."

Jacob said, "No! Please! . . . Accept the gift I give you. I am very happy to see your face again. It is like seeing the face of God because you have accepted me. So I beg you to accept the gift I give you. God has been

Jacob had not seen Esau for 20 years. Although it appears that Jacob was behaving as if he still had a guilty conscience for having cheated Esau, Esau seems to have forgiven him—maybe only moments earlier.

Jacob felt an emptiness he had not experienced since Laban had cheated him out of Rachel. But this was worse, because it was so final. *Oh, Mother,* he thought, *how much we have paid for that one day of deception! I'm sure you never thought that the day I left home would be the last time we'd ever see each other!*

Esau broke the silence. "Let us get going. I will travel with you."

"My master, you know that the children are weak. And I must be careful with my flocks and their young ones. . . . So, my master, you go on ahead of me, your servant. I will follow you slowly. . . . I will meet you, my master, in Edom."

"Then let me leave some of my men with you," Esau offered. Surely Jacob and his group could use the protection that some of Esau's workers could offer.

"No, thank you. I only want to please you, my master," Jacob replied.[8]

---

very good to me. And I have more than I need." And because Jacob begged, Esau accepted the gift.

Then Esau said, "Let us get going. I will travel with you."

But Jacob said to him, "My master, you know that the children are weak. And I must be careful with my flocks and their young ones. If I force them to go too far in one day, all the animals will die. So, my master, you go on ahead of me, your servant. I will follow you slowly. I will let the animals and the children set the speed at which we travel. I will meet you, my master, in Edom."

So Esau said, "Then let me leave some of my men with you."

"No, thank you," said Jacob. "I only want to please you, my master." So that day Esau started back to Edom. But Jacob went to Succoth. There he built a house for himself. And he made shelters for his animals.

Jacob lived in Shechem for a number of years—until his family wore out its welcome. The city was important in the early history of God's people, and several significant events took place in the region.

TODD BOLEN/BIBLEPLACES.COM

Once again the two men embraced and said goodbye. Jacob watched with a strange feeling of sadness as Esau and his 400 men disappeared into the distance. Esau turned for an instant and raised one arm in farewell.

As the years passed, Jacob's sons grew wild and willful, but God still loved Jacob and his family. Once more God spoke to him. "Go to the city of Bethel and live there. Make an altar to the God who appeared to you there."[9]

Jacob wanted to meet God again at Bethel. This time he would not be a lonely runaway. And this time he would bring his whole big family with him to worship.

Jacob called his family together. He looked sternly at his sons as he said, "We are going to Bethel to wor-

ship God. I will build an altar to Him who helped me in the time of my trouble and who has been with me everywhere I have gone. Put away the foreign gods you have."

Jacob's sons looked guiltily at one another. They still had gods from their grandfather's house. Other members of the family dropped their eyes in shame also. Some scurried to their tents and pulled out their little statues and idols.

"Bring them all over here under this tree!" Jacob commanded as he stood under a big oak. Men and women and even boys and girls dumped their little idols from Haran in a glittering, jangling pile under the tree. "Now bury them!" Jacob ordered. This place had special meaning for Jacob because it was here, some 20 years earlier, that God had appeared to him and blessed him.

As Jacob and his family bowed before the altar at Bethel, God once more spoke to Jacob in great love. "Your name is Jacob. But you will not be called Jacob any longer. Your new name will be Israel. . . . You will be the ancestor of many nations and kings. I gave Abraham and Isaac land. I will give that same land to you and your descendants."[10]

With solemn joy Jacob poured olive oil and wine upon a stone in the very place God had appeared to him so many years ago. "Surely this place is a dwelling place of God—Bethel!" he exclaimed. And softly, to himself, he murmured, "And at this place I am twice blessed!"

[1] Genesis 33:5, ICB.
[2] Verse 5, ICB.
[3] Verse 8, ICB.
[4] Verse 8, ICB.
[5] Verse 9, ICB.
[6] Verse 10, ICB.
[7] Verse 11, ICB.
[8] Verses 12-15, ICB.
[9] Genesis 35:1, ICB.
[10] Verses 10-12, ICB.

Forgiven and Twice Blessed!

Jacob smiled as he limped forward. "God is with us," he said. "Today I will see Esau!"

Soon they saw the army of 400 men coming toward them. A tall man walked at the front. "It's Esau!" Jacob said. "Look! His red hair is turning gray."

Jacob bowed low seven times before Esau.

Suddenly Esau ran straight at Jacob! Rachel gasped, "Will Esau hurt Jacob?"

Esau didn't hurt Jacob. Instead he hugged Jacob in his big arms. They kissed and then cried.

"I haven't seen you for 20 years," Esau said.

"God has been good to me," Jacob said. "And I will be your servant."

Esau smiled. "Jacob, who are all these people?"

"These are my wives and children," Jacob said. Everyone bowed to Esau, even Jacob and Rachel's young son, Joseph.

"Why did you send all those animals to me?" Esau asked.

"They're a present for you," Jacob said.

"I don't need them," Esau said.

"You must keep them," Jacob begged. "I want you to forgive me."

"My brother!" Esau said. "Thank you."

The twins talked for a long time. Jacob learned that his father, Isaac, was still alive, but his mother had died years earlier. Finally Esau returned home, allowing Jacob's family to follow at a slower speed.

As the years passed, Jacob's sons grew wild and strong, but God still loved them all. God spoke to Jacob and told him to worship at the city of Bethel.

"You must all throw away your idols," Jacob told his family firmly. "We are going to worship the true God." Jacob buried the idols under a tree.

When Jacob and his family worshipped God at Bethel, God spoke to Jacob. "Your name is not Jacob—Grabber—anymore," God said. "You are Israel—One Who Has Power With God."

—HEATHER GROVET

PETRA

Esau, Jacob's brother, was also called Edom, and Edom came to refer to the desert area where he lived. Today the best-known part of ancient Edom is the city of Petra, the kingdom of Jordan's most famous sightseeing spot. Originally occupied as early as 6500 B.C., this ancestral home of the Edomites had been taken

Daniel Frese/BiblePlaces.com

Left: Goats frolic in front of Ad Deir, a tomb sometimes called a monastery.

Below: Petra's amphitheater, cut out of solid rock, could seat more than 8,500 spectators.

Daniel Frese/BiblePlaces.com

over by the Nabateans by the end of the fourth century B.C. These spice traders carved buildings from the colorful sandstone.

The Siq, trail to Petra, winds through colorful limestone cliffs for about a mile, making the defense of Petra relatively easy.

BIBLE GLOSSARY/DICTIONARY

Here is a list of the biblical people and places mentioned in this book. The glossary not only gives information about each person and place, but also provides two guides that use easy-to-understand pronunciation apparatus. When a syllable is given in all CAPITAL letters, that is the syllable you put the stress on.

The first pronunciation offered is how most people who speak American English say the name. The second pronunciation is truly special. It tells you how to pronounce the name in Hebrew, Egyptian, Persian, Babylonian, Aramaic, or Greek. You will now know how, for instance, Eli pronounced Samuel's name when he called him! We give special thanks to Leona G. Running, expert in ancient Near Eastern languages, for preparing the pronunciation guides.

Have fun reading about these fascinating people and places of long ago. And enjoy the edge you'll have when it comes to biblical trivia, because you will be able to pronounce those tongue-twisting names just as they were spoken in the ancient Near East.

ABRAHAM—*American English pronunciation: AY-bra-ham. Hebrew pronunciation: av-ra-HAHM.* The name Abraham means "father of a multitude." Born in the city of Ur, he lived in the city of Haran until his father, Terah, died. Then God told him to leave for an unknown land—the "promised land"—Canaan. God covenanted with Abraham, promising to give him land and descendants and making him a blessing to the world. When Abraham was 100 years old, Isaac was born. Abraham died at 175 years of age. Scripture refers to him as a friend of God (2 Chronicles

Abraham

20:7; cf. Isaiah 41:8). Scholars differ as to when he lived—during the Early Bronze Age or the Middle Bronze Age. Abraham is an important figure for Judaism, Christianity, and Islam.

BASEMATH—*American English pronunciation: BAS-e-math; Hebrew pronunciation: bah-se-MATH.* The name means "balsam" or "balm." The Old Testament refers to two or three women with this name. (It all depends on how one interprets the biblical evidence.) It appears that Esau married two women by this name. One was the daughter of Elon, a Hittite. The other was the daughter of Ishmael. This latter Basemath gave birth to a baby boy named Reuel, which was also one of the names for Moses' father-in-law.

BEER-SHEBA—*American English pronunciation: beer-SHEE-bah; Hebrew pronunciation: bee-air-SHEH-vah.* The name means "well of seven," which most likely refers to the seven lambs that Abraham gave to King Abimelech in order to maintain peaceful water rights. Abraham had the well in

Beer-sheba

question dug. Later Isaac also made a treaty with Abimelech regarding water rights. Beer-sheba was the southernmost town in the kingdom of Israel, as in the common expression "from Dan to Beer-sheba." (Dan was the northernmost city.) During the time of the prophet Amos it seems that a cult center—temple or shrine—existed here. Archaeologists have uncovered rocks that had formed an altar there and reconstructed it. When Sarah sent her pregnant maidservant, Hagar, away from the camp, God met her at the

Beer-sheba well. Much later Samuel's two wicked sons served as judges here. The city was destroyed by King Sennacherib around 700 B.C. The modern city of Beer-sheba is a thriving city that houses Ben-Gurion University of the Negev. The current city may be located atop the ancient site of Abraham's Beer-sheba. It's about three miles from the modern city of Tell es-Saba', which has been excavated in part by Y. Aharoni and Z. Herzog. In 1990 efforts to reconstruct the old city of Beer-sheba as it

Traditional site of Jacob's ladder at Bethel.

Jacob later had a dream about God's presence while he was fleeing from home (and from his brother Esau) while he was on the way to Uncle Laban's place in Mesopotamia. During the time of the judges the ark of the covenant was situated in Bethel. The prophet Samuel performed some of his administrative duties here, and during the time of Elijah a school of the prophets was located here. Bethel still exists as modern Beitîn.

BETHUEL—*American pronunciation: be-THOO-el. Hebrew pronunciation: bee-thoo-AIL.* Bethuel means either "man of God" or "house of God." In the Old Testament the name was given to a man and to a town. In this book Bethuel refers to the man, the son of Nahor and Milcah, and Abraham's nephew. He was the father of Laban and Rebekah. Scripture refers to him as an Aramean. This means he lived in Paddan-aram, a confederation of at least 40 tribes in northwestern Mesopotamia, between the Khabur and Euphrates rivers. Laban rather than Bethuel played the major role in Rebekah's betrothal to Isaac.

stood during the time of King Hezekiah began.

BETHEL—*American English pronunciation: BETH-el. Hebrew pronunciation: bayth-AIL.* The city of Bethel, originally called Luz, was an important religious center in Canaan and is 11 miles north of Jerusalem. The name means "house of God." (There was even a northwest Semitic god by the name of Bethel, who was supposed to be one of the sons of Uranos [Heaven] and Ge [Earth]. Some evidence points to the possibility that the word also referred to stones that were superstitiously regarded as being alive.) Archaeological evidence points to inhabitants in the area as far back as possibly 3200 B.C., but the city itself was probably founded around 2000 B.C. The city is close to the town of Ai. Other than the city of Jerusalem, Bethel is the place most often mentioned in the Old Testament. At one point in its history, the city had walls that were 11 feet thick. Abraham in his wanderings in Canaan lived there on at least two occasions. It is where

It may be that this was a matrilineal family in which the brother rather than the father had the authority to give the sister in marriage. Other scholars speculate that perhaps Bethuel had already died or was in some way mentally or physically incapacitated. In certain ancient texts (from the city of Nuzi in Mesopotamia, a brother made the arrangements for a sister's marriage.)

BILHAH—*American English pronunciation: BIL-hah. Hebrew pronunciation: bil-HAH.* Bilhah, the name may mean "not worried," referred to both a woman and a town in the Old Testament. In this book this proper noun refers to Rachel's maidservant and Jacob's concubine. Laban gave Bilhah to Jacob as a secondary wife or concubine. This was in harmony with Mesopotamian practice, which allowed a barren wife to give her servant girl to her husband in order to raise up an heir. Bilhah gave birth to Dan and Naphtali.

CANAAN/CANAANITES—*American English pronunciation: KAY-nan. Hebrew*

Bethuel

pronunciation: ke-NA-an. Canaan is the equivalent of Palestine—the area between the Mediterranean Sea and the Jordan River. The people who lived there are called Canaanites and were descendants of Ham's son, Noah's grandson, by the same name. Canaan was first referred to in written documents around 2300 B.C., but archaeologists say that they have uncovered evidence of civilization there dating back to 3000 B.C. The Canaanite city known as Ugarit had a library (perhaps for priests), which archaeologists have discovered. The language of Canaan was absorbed by Abraham's descendants, becoming the language now known as biblical Hebrew.

DAMASCUS—*American English pronunciation: da-MASS-kus. Hebrew pronunciation: dam-MESS-ek.* The city of Damascus is arguably the world's oldest continuously inhabited city and still exists—as the capital of modern Syria. According to the Jewish historian Josephus, the city was founded by one of Shem's grandsons. It was the capital of ancient Aram from the tenth to the eighth centuries B.C. The city is situated on the banks of the Barada River (ancient Abana River) and on a plateau some 2,200 feet above sea level. The city itself forms part of the oasis of Ghuta, which is pretty much on the edge of the desert. In ancient times its patron deity was Hadad, a storm and fertility god. The city was famous for its gardens and orchards, and its wine was well known throughout the ancient Near East. The fabric that today we call "damask" comes from the name of this city, where this special cloth originated.

DEAD SEA (SEA OF SALT in Hebrew)—*American English pronunciation: DEDD SEE. Hebrew pronunciation: yahm ham-MEH-lakh.* Also called the Salt Sea, Sea of the Arabah, Sea of the Plain, and the Eastern Sea. It is the biggest lake in Palestine (nearly 50 miles long and 6 to 10 miles wide) and the lowest body of water anywhere on earth—1,320 feet below sea level. Each day the Dead Sea takes in more than 6 million tons of water from the Jordan River (other rivers and streams also flow into it), but the lake

has no outlet. The area gets an average of 330 full days of sunshine annually, so evaporation makes the water very dense with 21 mineral salts. (Its salinity is 25 to 28 percent, in contrast with 4 to 6 percent salinity of ocean water, making it the saltiest body of water in the world.) At the bottom and around the edges of the Dead Sea, salt precipitates out and piles up. Only a few fish can live here, but only near its inlets. From 1947 to 1956 more than 800 scrolls were found in nearby caves. These scrolls come from an area

known as Qumran, the location of a group of Essenes, an ascetic cult of Judaism. There are biblical and nonbiblical scrolls in the findings. They are written in Hebrew or Aramaic and were hidden sometime between A.D. 66 and 70. The biblical Dead Sea scrolls (usually abbreviated DSS) are the oldest biblical manuscripts available to scholars. Some contain psalms of David that were not preserved in the Judeo-Christian Bible. The DSS have given biblical scholars many insights into the culture and language of turn-of-the-era Judaism.

Dead Sea shoreline

DEBORAH—*American English pronunciation: DEB-o-rah. Hebrew: de-vo-RAH.* The name Deborah means "bee." In the Old Testament two women had that name. The person referred to in this book was Rebekah's nurse, who went with her to Canaan, where Rebekah married Isaac, whom she had not met. When Deborah died at Bethel, she was with Jacob's family. The oak (terebinth) tree shading her grave was named *Allon-bacuth,* which means "oak of weeping." Scholars speculate that this was possibly a sacred spot.

DINAH—*American English pronunciation: DIE-nah. Hebrew pronunciation: dee-NAH.* This feminine name probably comes from the Hebrew root for "to judge." It may mean "justice" or "judged." We do not know much about Dinah, the seventh child of Jacob and Leah. She was also Leah's last child. After Leah gave birth to Dinah, Rachel's infertility changed, and she gave birth to Joseph and then Benjamin. The name also appears in cuneiform documents, which refer to a maidservant by that name in the city of Gozan, Mesopotamia.

Dinah

JACK PENNINGTON

EDOM—*American English pronunciation: EE-dum. Hebrew pronunciation: eh-DOHM.* Not only was Edom another name for Esau but also it came to refer to the area where Esau lived. (The people who lived in this area were called Edomites.) The name means "red" and may refer to the color of Esau's hair and/or complexion as well as to the red soil and rocks in part of the geographical area. Edom was situated southeast and southwest of the Dead Sea and covered a territory roughly 100 miles long and 20 miles wide. The area was also known in the Old Testament as Seir and Sela. From Hellenistic times it came to be known as Idumea. The Old Testament has Esau and his descendants moving into the area. They were not the first inhabitants there, however. Prior to that time a people known as Horites lived there. Scholars who do not hold to a short chronology find evidence for people living in the area as far back as 500,000 years ago. No written records by the ancient Edomites have been discovered.

The earliest mention of Edom that we know of is in Egyptian Papyrus Anastasi, which was written between 1224 and 1214 B.C. It mentions allowing Edomite nomads entrance to the eastern part of the Nile Delta. The famous King's Highway road ran through Edom. Much of Edom was mountainous and high desert, but two small areas were suited to agriculture. Also, copper was mined in Edom. The Edomites were seminomadic Bedouins and were sometimes referred to in Scripture as "brothers" to the Israelites, although the relationship between the two groups was typically marked with hostility. King David conquered the Edomites, but much later they regained their independence. The Babylonians later conquered Edom, and at the same time a group known as Nabataeans moved into the area. Of the Edomites Diodorus Siculus wrote: "They have no poor amongst their kind, they honor the meek and dispossessed, and value mercy, peace, and forgiveness." He reported that "the women are treated as equal" to the men. Around the end of the second century

Eliezer

B.C., John Hyrcanus I conquered them and forced the men to be circumcised, thus the Nabataeans became Jews and were called Idumeans. Herod the Great was an Idumean. The famous city of Petra was carved into the red sandstone within the territory of Edom. Qaus was an Edomite god.

ELIEZER—*American English pronunciation: el-ee-EE-zer. Hebrew pronunciation: el-ee-EH-zer.* The name Eliezer means "my God is a helper." The Bible mentions

11 different men with this name. The Eliezer referred to in this book was Abraham's servant, apparently born in Abraham's own household but with ancestors from Damascus. If Abraham had not had any sons, by ancient custom Eliezer would have become his heir. Abraham sent Eliezer to Haran to find a wife for Isaac—Rebekah.

ESAU—*American English pronunciation: EE-saw. Hebrew: ay-SOW.* Esau was Jacob's twin brother, born shortly ahead of Jacob himself, to Isaac and Rebekah. The meaning of the name is obscure. The Hebrew word for hairy is *se'ar*. The name Esau appears outside Scripture in the non-biblical Ebla records, but it does not refer to the biblical Esau. Esau also went by the name Edom, which comes from a root meaning "red." According to the biblical account, Esau was the ancestor of the Edomites (later known as the Idumeans). Esau liked to hunt, whereas Jacob preferred caring for sheep. Isaac showed partiality toward his son Esau, who married Adah, Basemath, and Oholibamah. Esau's sons were Eliphaz, Reuël, Jeush, Jalam, and Korah. When Esau and his family moved into the high desert area known as Edom, they drove out the Horites who were living there.

EUPHRATES—*American English pronunciation: yew-FRAY-teez. Hebrew pronunciation: pe-RAHTH.* This was one of the two rivers between which on the alluvial plain was located the land of Mesopotamia. The present name comes from Greek. The river has gone by the following names: *Buranunu* (Sumerian), *Purattu* (Akkadian), *Perath*

(Hebrew), *Ufratu* (ancient Persian), *Al-Furât* (Arabic), and *Firat* (Turkish). Beginning in eastern Turkey, it flows for nearly 1,800 miles into the Persian Gulf. Each year some 990 billion cubic feet of water flows through the Euphrates, one of the most important rivers in the world. During the months of April and May the volume of water is greatest because of snowmelt. Xenophon said that the river turned the desert into "a garden of fertility." The alluvial plain area produces crops such as dates and wheat.

Throughout the millennia, the course of the river has shifted, but at one time or another the cities Mari, Sippar, Nippur, Shurrupak, Uruk, Ur, Eridu, Carchemish, and Babylon were along its banks. In fact, the Euphrates flowed right through the center of Babylon. In the Bible we first learn of the Euphrates in the book of Genesis, which lists the river as one of four rivers watering the Garden of Eden. Because of Noah's flood, the current course of the Euphrates might be in quite a different location from the Euphrates River in

Euphrates

Haran

Qarqar. After varying fortunes, it fell in 720 B.C. to Sargon II, who deported many of its citizens and brought in people from Samaria. It was here that Nebuchadnezzar judged rebellious King Zedekiah, last monarch of Judah, and executed his sons. Modern Hama is home for nearly 300,000 people. It is a market center for crops grown in the vicinity—cotton, wheat, barley, millet, and corn. One can still see in the Orontes River "nouria," large waterwheels (some up to 90 feet in diameter) that were used for irrigation purposes.

HARAN—*American English pronunciation: HAY-ran. Hebrew pronunciation: hah-RAHN.* Haran was a very old city in northern Mesopotamia and appears to have been founded in the mid-third millennium B.C. The root behind the name probably meant something like "road," "crossroads," or even "business trip." Haran was an important religious and political center early on. It and the ancient city of Ur, which was in southern Mesopotamia, were centers of worship of the moon god Sin. About the time that Terah and his family left ancient Ur and

the Garden of Eden. We just don't know. Often the Old Testament writers refer to it simply as "the river."

GREAT SEA—*See Mediterranean Sea.*

HAMATH—*American English pronunciation: HAY-math. Hebrew pronunciation: ha-MAHTH.* The name means "citadel" or "fortress." This city-state (now the Syrian city of Hama) is located on the Orontes River in the Valley of Lebanon. It was to be part of the northern boundary of

Israel. Earliest references to the city by name come from tablets found at Ebla. According to the findings of Danish archaeologists, the city was inhabited as far back as the fourth millennium B.C. Although Aramaeans lived there, archaeological findings indicate that at one point in its history the Hittites lived there. The city deity was Ashima. King David had friendly relationships with Hamath. In 853 B.C. Hamath provided 700 chariots, 700 cavalry, and 10,000 foot soldiers in a fight against Assyrian King Shalmaneser III at moved to Haran the Elamites had destroyed Ur. In fact, that may have been the reason Terah took the long trip north from Ur to Haran, where Terah died. After Terah's death, when Abram was 75 years old, Abram and his immediate family left Haran for the Promised Land. Later Isaac and Rebekah sent Jacob to Haran to find refuge from his angry brother Esau. There Jacob lived with Uncle Laban and married his cousins Rachel and Leah. Many hundreds of years later Haran was the last capital of the Assyrian Empire.

Nabonidus, the last native Babylonian king, reconstructed the temple to the moon god Sin in Haran and made his mother its high priest.

HEBRON—*American English pronunciation: HEE-bron. Hebrew pronunciation: hev-ROHN.* This word can refer to both a place and a person. In this book it is used only of the place. Hebron was an important city in the hill country, with an altitude of 3,350 feet above sea level. It is situated about 20 miles from Jerusalem and was originally

known as Kiriath-arba. The city was situated on some major trade routes. The ancient site is today known as *Jebel er-Rumeidah*. Abraham lived in the vicinity of Hebron for some time, and here he bought the Cave of Machpelah, where he, Sarah, Isaac, Rebekah, Jacob, and Leah were buried. Some have pointed out that this was the first Jewish purchase of real estate in Israel. Nearly 2,000 years later Herod the Great constructed an enclosure around the burial site, and parts of the wall still stand inside the church (built during the Byzantine Period) that now marks the spot. There is a modern city called Hebron that is situated nearby the ancient site. Modern Hebron is sometimes called *el-Khalil*, which in Arabic means "the Friend," a take-off on Abraham's title in Scripture "Friend of God."

HITTITE—*American English pronunciation: HIT-tite. Hebrew pronunciation: hit-TEE.* The word seems to refer to two distinct, though perhaps distantly related, people. The Hittites mentioned in this book lived in the land of Canaan and were descendants

Hebron: view to southwest with mosque of Abraham (center).

of Noah's son Ham through Ham's son Canaan. These Hittites lived in Canaan prior to the time of Abraham. They had settled largely on the central ridge of Judah in the area of the city of Hebron. It is possible that the similarity of their name to that of the Japhethite Hittites in Syria is coincidental. The personal names of the Canaanite Hittites mentioned in the Bible are definitely not Indo-European, as are those names used of Hittites in Syria. Abraham purchased the Cave of Machpelah from the Canaanite Hittites, and after the exodus from Egypt and during the conquest of Canaan, the Israelites never did wipe out the Hittites, who remained in the land—even in the area of Jerusalem—for many centuries. These people can be called "the sons of Heth." On the other hand, the Japhethite Hittites who lived in the area of Syria were often known as the "men of Hatti." These people of the Hittite Empire invaded the area of Syria and formed the empire around 1880 B.C. They were of Indo-European origin and took over the land where the non-Indo-European Hattians lived. The empire reached its zenith under King Suppiluliumas I (c. 1375-c. 1335 B.C.). It collapsed as an important imperial presence around 1200 B.C. under the invasion of the "Sea Peoples," although fragments of the people continued for many more centuries and were called inhabitants of "Hatti-land" by the Babylonians. These Japhethite Hittites spoke at least eight different Indo-European languages, which were written in cuneiform. The early Hittite kings were not nearly as despotic as their contemporary ancient Near Eastern rulers. The kings were considered to be head of the clergy, and when they died they purportedly became gods. The Hittites worshipped 1,000 deities, who were quite mobile and not attached to a particular geographical location. The Hittites raised crops and cattle.

ISAAC—*American English pronunciation: EYE-zak. Hebrew pronunciation: yits-HAHKH.* The name Isaac means "he laughs." He was the son of Abraham and Sarah, the child God promised through

Isaac

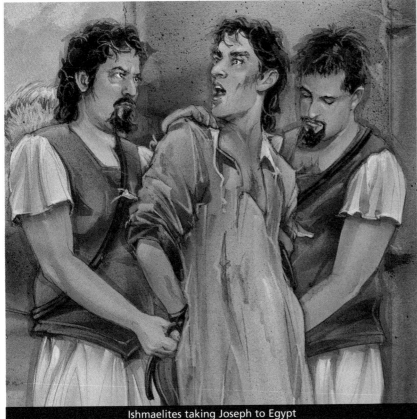

Ishmaelites taking Joseph to Egypt

whom the whole world would be blessed. Because of Sarah's barrenness, they had just about given up on the idea they would have a child. Sarah's pregnancy was considered miraculous and a direct result of God's promises to them. Abraham was 100 years old and Sarah 90 when Isaac was born. They had entered Canaan 25 years before Isaac's birth. Isaac married Rebekah, and they had two sons—Jacob and Esau. For a while Isaac lived at a place called Gerar, where God renewed with Isaac the covenant He had

originally made with Abraham. From Gerar Isaac moved to Beer-sheba. He was 180 years old when he died.

ISHMAELITES—*American English pronunciation: ISH-ma-e-lights. Hebrew pronunciation: yish-me-ay-LEEM.* God promised that Ishmael, the first son born to Abraham in Canaan, would be the ancestor of a great nation. Genesis 16:12 says that Ishmael would be "a wild ass of a man" (RSV). This was not really an insult. Rather it described the way of life that his descendants would take

up—a freely roaming nomadic lifestyle. Ishmael married an Egyptian woman, and they had 12 sons or princes of as many tribes. The names of the 12 sons are: Nebaioth, Kedar, Adbeel, Mibsam (or Mishma), Dumah, Massa, Hadad, Tema, Jetur, Naphish, and Kedemah. This last son is the only one of his descendants not mentioned by name in nonbiblical ancient Near Eastern sources. According to the *Anchor Bible Dictionary*, the Ishmaelites were the "first central North Arabian desert power to appear in history" (vol. 3, p. 517). The Ishmaelites became famous for their skillful use of the bow and arrow. There is evidence in Scripture that the Ishmaelites and Midianites were of the same ethnic group. Many modern Arabs regard themselves as Ishmael's offspring.

ISRAEL—*American English pronunciation: IZ-rah-ell. Hebrew pronunciation: yis-rah-AYL.* Israel was the new covenant name that God gave Jacob after their wrestling bout by the Jabbok River. Throughout the Old Testament it is often used interchangeably with Jacob. The word also can refer to the entire group of Jacob's descendants, who are also called the Israelites. When the monarchy was divided after King Solomon's death, Israel referred to the 10 northern tribes that broke away from the Davidic monarchy in 931 B.C.

ISSACHAR—*American English pronunciation: ISS-a-car. Hebrew pronunciation: yis-sah-KAHR.* This masculine name means "there is hire" or "man for hire." The Old Testament mentions two men with this name. The Issachar in this book is Jacob's ninth son and Leah's fifth son. The circumstances surrounding his birth are interesting—some might say bizarre. Leah, who had given birth to several children, suddenly found herself barren—a condition that had plagued her sister Rachel, of whom Jacob was especially fond. When Leah's oldest son, Reuben, came home with some mandrakes that he had found, Rachel immediately asked for them. (Mandrakes were considered to enhance fertility.) Leah told Rachel that she could have the mandrakes on one condition—Leah would spend the night with Jacob. The deal was struck, Leah

Jabbok fords

slept with Jacob, and soon Leah found herself pregnant with Issachar. Issachar was the ancestor of the Israelite tribe of Issachar. The Bible tells us very little about this son of Jacob who had four sons. The royal city of Jezreel, where King Ahab and Queen Jezebel built a winter palace, was located in the territory allotted to the tribe of Issachar. Also several important battles took place within the territory of Issachar.

JABBOK—*American English pronunciation: JAB-ock. Hebrew pronunciation: yah-BOHK.* The Jabbok River, one of the four major streams flowing through the Transjordan, is a tributary of the Jordan River. Its name may mean "flowing," but its modern Arabic name, *Nahr ez-Zerqā,* means "blue river." The Jabbok begins near Amman, Jordan, which in Bible times was called Rabbath-ammon. That area receives 28 to 32 inches of rain each year, which makes the Jabbok a good source of water. After flowing some 50 to 60 miles, it joins the Jordan River about 25 miles north of the Dead Sea. In the hill country through which it flows, the banks of the Jabbok are lined with oleander shrubs, which have colorful blossoms. One branch of the Jabbok formed the border of King Sihon's realm, and another branch separated Sihon's territory from that ruled by King Og of Bashan. It was here near Penuel that Jacob spent a night wrestling with God. The precise location is not known, although some scholars speculate that Penuel may be what is now known as Tulul edh-Dhahab near Succoth. The valley through which the Jabbok flowed also served as a main travel route in the ancient Near East, and when Gideon routed the Midianites, he and his soldiers chased them up through the Jabbok River valley.

JACOB—*American English pronunciation: JAY-cob. Hebrew pronunciation: yah-a-KOHV.* The Bible mentions two men by the name of Jacob—one in the Old Testament and the other in the New Testament. The Jacob featured in this book is the Old Testament Jacob, son of Isaac and Rebekah and twin of Esau. The name as it now stands means "heel grabber" or "supplanter." Some scholars speculate that perhaps the name was originally *ya ʿqōb-il*, which means "May God protect" or perhaps Jacob-el, which means "may God supplant." Jacob, whose name was later changed to Israel, was the progenitor of the Hebrew (Israelite) people. He had one daughter, Dinah, and 12 sons, from whom the names of the 12 Hebrew tribes were derived. Jacob, along with his father Isaac and grandfather Abraham received God's promise of covenant blessings. Jacob, unlike his hunter brother, Esau, was a quiet person who enjoyed herding flocks. Rebekah favored Jacob, whereas Esau was Isaac's favorite son. Esau sold his birthright to Jacob for a meal of lentils, and later Jacob, under Rebekah's prodding, impersonated Esau when Isaac, who was blind and ill at age 137, wanted to give Esau what he felt was his final blessing before his death. Esau grew so enraged at Jacob's deceit that he threatened to murder him. Jacob, now 77 years old, fled to Haran in Mesopotamia, where he lived with Uncle Laban for 20 years. When Jacob, now Israel, returned to Canaan, he took up residence in Succoth, Shechem,

Jacob

and then Bethel. When he was 130 years old, Jacob moved to Egypt, where his long-lost son Joseph was vizier to the pharaoh during a time of severe famine. He lived in Egypt for 17 years and died at age 147. He was later buried in the Cave of Machpelah, which Abraham had purchased when Sarah died.

JERUSALEM—*American English pronunciation: je-ROO-sa-lem. Hebrew pronunciation: yay-roo-sha-LAH-yim. Greek pronunciation: yay-ro-SAHL-yoo-ma; ye-roo-sa-LEM.* The city of Jerusalem is honored by three major world religions—Judaism, Christianity, and Islam. The city is situated on two ridges about 2,500 feet above sea level. The climate is quite arid because the city lies at the edge of the Judean desert. Historically, the city relied on a single spring of water—the Gihon, which provided a continuous supply of water. Although the name of this famous biblical city has been interpreted to mean "city of peace," it most likely means "foundation of [the god] Salem." Archaeologists have found pottery that they believe dates all the way back to 3500 B.C., and settlements here date

back to the Early Bronze Age. The earliest reference to "Salim" is found in the texts found at Ebla (dating c. 2400 B.C.). During the nineteenth century B.C. the Egyptians referred to it as *Rushalimum*. The tablets found at el-Amarna (fourteenth century B.C.) call it *Urusalim*. During the Middle Bronze Age, Jerusalem became a walled city. During the eleventh century B.C., the Jebusites lived here in a city of 11 acres. They said that the city was so secure against invaders that even blind and lame men could defend it (2 Samuel 5:6).

When David became king of the united monarchy, he decided to move his capital from Hebron to Jerusalem, but the city was not yet under his control. So he besieged it, and Joab and his brave men climbed up its water shaft and captured the city for Israel. At that time the city covered no more than 15 acres and housed some 2,000 people. King Solomon, David's son, enlarged the city to 32 acres, with an estimated population of no more than 5,000 inhabitants. King Hezekiah expanded the city to 125 acres, with a population of around 25,000. The

Jerusalem

Babylonian army destroyed Jerusalem in 586 B.C. The Roman general Pompey captured Jerusalem in 63 B.C. In 54 B.C. Crassus plundered the Temple, and in 40 B.C. the Parthians looted the city, but three years later Herod the Great took back the city and began extensive repairs. Herod expanded Jerusalem so that it sprawled over 230 acres, with an estimated populace of 40,000 persons. In A.D. 66 the Jews rebelled against Rome, and in A.D. 70 Roman forces numbering 80,000 besieged Jerusalem under Titus. From early May to late July of that year more than 100,000 Jews died in the city. Finally the Roman army captured Jerusalem and burned the Temple. The Jewish historian Josephus claims that the total Jewish casualties of this war amounted to more than 1 million Jews dead and 97,000 Jewish prisoners of war. In A.D. 132 the Jews again revolted. Under their leader, Bar Cocheba, they claimed to have set up a city independent of Rome. This short-lived "government" even minted its own coins. The Roman armies squelched the rebellion in A.D. 135. The city was renamed

Jordan River entering the Sea of Galilee

Aelia Capitolina, and a temple to Jupiter was built on the site of Herod's Temple. Any Jews who set foot inside the city were to be executed.

JORDAN (river)—*American English pronunciation: JOR-dan. Hebrew pronunciation: yar-DAYN. Greek pronunciation: yor-DAH-nays.* The Hebrew word may mean "descender," an apt description of the river that begins with four streams forming in the snow fields of Mount Hermon and ends up flowing through Palestine through Lake Huleh,

then the Sea of Galilee, and finally to the Dead Sea, which has no outlet. The Jordan is the world's lowest river, most of the time flowing below sea level. Because the Jordan River is so twisting, it flows for 135 miles to cover the linear 65 miles between the Sea of Galilee and the Dead Sea, which is 1,300 feet below sea level, the lowest surface on our planet. The river runs from two to 10 feet in depth and divides Palestine into the land of Canaan (sometimes called Cisjordan) west of the river and the Transjordan east of the river. The river itself

Joseph

it—the miracle being the opportunity to cross dry-shod and not the mechanics of how the river happened to dry up.

JOSEPH—*American English pronunciation: JOE-zeff. Hebrew pronunciation: yoh-SAYF.* Fourteen different men in the Bible share the name Joseph, which in Hebrew means "may he add." The Old Testament Joseph featured in this book was the son of Jacob and Rachel. Jacob was 91 years old when Joseph was born, and had served Laban for 14 years—six years before the family moved back to Canaan. Jacob especially favored Joseph and made him a special garment that was the envy of Joseph's brothers. When Joseph began having dreams in which his brothers and other family members gave him great deference, the jealousy became even more vitriolic. When Jacob sent 17-year-old Joseph to find his brothers, who had taken the flocks to Shechem and then to Dothan, the brothers ripped off his coat, threw Joseph into a dry well, and ultimately sold him to Midianite traders for 20 silver shekels. They smeared blood over Joseph's

contains an average of 20 billion cubic feet of water annually above the Sea of Galilee. Below that an average of 17 billion cubic feet of water is added to the river. During droughts the average annual flow can drop to 8 billion cubic feet of water, and during especially wet periods the flow increases to as much as 35 billion cubic feet of water per year. The Jordan Valley is the strip of land along the river between the Sea of Galilee and the Dead Sea. In ancient times there were no bridges across the river, so people had to find fords or ride boats across it. The

children of Israel miraculously crossed the flooded Jordan and into the Promised Land on dry ground. Historically earthquakes have dammed up the river for short periods of time. For instance, on the night of December 8, A.D. 1267, a pile of debris fell into the river and blocked its flow for 16 hours. Similar events occurred in 1546, 1906, and 1927. On July 11, 1927, the river was dammed by debris for 21.5 hours. Some biblical students think that God used a similar natural means in drying up the river when the Israelites miraculously crossed coat and tore it so that Jacob would think Joseph had been attacked, killed, and eaten by a wild animal—perhaps a lion. In Egypt Joseph was sold to Potiphar. Later accused of sexual assault by Potiphar's wife, Joseph ended up in prison. Thirteen years later he was released when he interpreted a dream for the pharaoh, who then made Joseph second in command in Egypt. Joseph married Asenath, daughter of the Egyptian priest at Heliopolis (also called On). He and Asenath had two boys—

Manasseh and Ephraim. Joseph gathered grain during seven years with bountiful harvest, and then dispersed the grain during seven years of devastating famine.

JUDAH—*American English pronunciation: JOO-dah. Hebrew pronunciation: ye-hoo-DAH.*

The Old Testament mentions six men with the name Judah, which may mean "let Him [God] be praised," but scholars are uncertain of the actual meaning. The full Hebrew form of the name is *Yehúdah*. The Judah mentioned in this book is Jacob's fourth son by Leah. Judah married Shua, a Canaanite woman, who bore him three sons—Er, Onan, and Shelah. Judah is the one who, to save Joseph's life, suggested that the brothers sell him to the Ishmaelites. It was not a particularly good option, but at least Judah spared Joseph's life, and God saw to it that in turn Joseph, as vizier of Egypt, was able later to spare his family's life by providing them with food during the terrible famine that wracked both Egypt and Canaan, an unusual occurrence because rarely did famine strike both geographical areas at the same time. When Jacob on his deathbed uttered blessings over his sons, he purposely bestowed the birthright blessing on Judah rather than on Reuben (Jacob's firstborn son) or on Simeon or Levi, both of whom were older than Judah himself. Judah was the progenitor of the tribe of Judah, perhaps the most important of the 12 Israelite tribes. Through his line King David and Jesus Christ were born. The name also came to refer to a geographical territory west of the Dead Sea in the Promised Land. Under the divided monarchy, Judah referred to the southern

Judah

political realm that was in contrast with the northern political division known as Israel. Later under Persian rule the name was applied to the province occupied by the Jews who had returned from the Babylonian exile.

JUDITH—*American English pronunciation: JOO-dith. Hebrew pronunciation: ye-hoo-DEETH.* This is the Hebrew feminine form of the name Judah and means the same thing: "let Him [God] be praised" or perhaps "Jewess," a female Judean even though

she herself was born to Beeri, a Hittite man. That her father is identified as a Hittite has puzzled biblical scholars. It is suggested that these Hittites were actually Canaanites who lived in the vicinity of Hebron and who were of different stock from the Anatolian Hittites, who were descendants of Japheth (and thus Indo-European) and who later appeared on the scene. Some scholars refer to these Semite Hittites as Proto-Hittites. Most of the Hittites mentioned in the Old Testament had Semitic rather than Hittite names, and Judith

Judith

is one of them. She was one of two Hittite wives (the other woman was Adah) whom Esau married. Isaac and Rebekah did not want their son Jacob to marry a Canaanite/Hittite woman and so sent him to Laban's place in Mesopotamia.

LABAN—*American English pronunciation: LAY-ban. Hebrew pronunciation: lah-VAHN.* Son of Bethuel, Laban, whose name means "white" or "pale," was the grandson of Abraham's brother Nahor. Genesis 29:5 calls him the son of Nahor, but scholars believe that the expression should be understood as "descendant of Nahor." (In the ancient Near East, the expression "son of . . ." could refer not to immediate parentage but to ancestry.) Laban lived in Haran in Paddan-aram, part of ancient Mesopotamia. Laban's sister was Rebekah, who became Isaac's wife. When Jacob later fled home because Esau wanted to kill him, he went to Haran and lived with Laban for 20 years. While there he married Leah and Rachel, Laban's daughters. From law texts found at the Hurrian city of Nuzi, some scholars have concluded that the *teraphim* that

Leah

Rachel "stole" and hid under the camel saddle were more than tribal gods. Possession of the *teraphim* is alleged to have given possession of the family's property. Laban, by "adopting" Jacob into his family, because he (Laban) had no male heirs, gave Jacob the right to own the *teraphim*. So what Rachel had done was not an illegal act but rather exerting her legal rights through Jacob to her father's property. Although there is biblical evidence that Laban honored Yahweh, there is also evidence that he worshipped pagan deities as well.

The practice of worshipping one god while believing that other gods also exist is called henotheism. Genesis 30:27 (RSV) seems to indicate that Laban practiced divination. Wherever Laban appears in the biblical account, he is portrayed as greedy and even dishonest.

LEAH—*American English pronunciation: LEE-uh. Hebrew pronunciation: lay-AH.* Leah was Laban's older daughter. The name means "wild cow" or "gazelle." Her father tricked Jacob into marrying her when he (Jacob) thought he was really marrying Rachel, Leah's younger sister. Leah and Jacob had six sons (Reuben, Simeon, Levi, Judah, Issachar, and Zebulun) and one daughter (Dinah). Her maidservant was Zilpah, whom her father gave to her as a wedding present. Some versions of the Bible say that she had "weak" eyes. It is possible that this expression was not really an insult but a compliment—that she had feminine eyes, soft eyes.

LEVI—*American English pronunciation: LEE-vie. Hebrew pronunciation: lay-VEE.* The name may mean "joined" or "attached" or "twisted." Four different people in Scripture went by that name. The Levi mentioned in this book was the third son that Jacob and Leah had. He was the progenitor of the tribe of Levi, from which the Jewish priests came. The Bible records only one event in his life—when he participated in the massacre of King Hamor, his son Shechem, and the men who lived in the city of Shechem. Shechem men had raped Dinah, Levi's sister. Then Shechem decided he wanted to marry Dinah. In fact, it appears that Dinah moved in with him. Levi and Simeon were incensed over what had happened, and when King Hamor and Shechem asked that Dinah marry Shechem, the two brothers hatched up a plan to get even. They told the Shechemites that if all the men in the city were circumcised, then they would let Dinah marry Shechem and that other marriages would also be allowed between the two groups. The king and his son agreed, and soon all the men living in Shechem had been circumcised. Several days later, when every male was still hurting and indisposed from the surgery, Levi and Simeon entered the city and killed all the men there. Levi had three sons: Gershon (or Gershom), Kohath, and Merari.

MAHANAIM—*American English pronunciation: may-ha-NAY-im. Hebrew pronunciation: maha-NAH-yim.* This place name most likely has a Hebrew dual ending and so means "two camps." It was located near where the Jabbok River joined the Jordan River. When Jacob had a vision of a multitude of protecting angels with him, he named the site Mahanaim—"two camps." In these early days the area was forested. The city by this name

Mediterranean Sea

was later given to the Merarite Levites to live in as their part of the Promised Land allotment. It also served as a city of refuge where people could flee for protection when they had accidentally killed someone and needed security from blood vengeance. For a short period of time Mahanaim was the capital city of northern Israel when Ish-bosheth, Saul's son, was king and David ruled only over Judah. Later, during Absalom's rebellion, King David fled here for a brief period of time. It was also just north of Mahanaim where Joab killed Absalom,

thereby ending his insurgence. The city is mentioned in Egypt on the temple of Amon at Karnak, reporting that Pharaoh Shishak had conquered and destroyed it. Its precise location and archaeological ruins are a matter of dispute, but a growing consensus among scholars favors Telul ed-Dhahab el-Garbi, an old site located atop a sandstone outcrop at a ford in the Jabbok River.

MEDITERRANEAN SEA—*American English pronunciation: meh-deh-ter-RAIN-ee-an-see. Hebrew pronunciation:*

(the Sea) ba-YAHM. The word "Mediterranean" is Latin for "in the midst of lands." In other words, the Mediterranean Sea is basically—though not entirely—landlocked. Estimates are that it takes a whole century for the entire water content to be replenished with new water from the Atlantic Ocean and through the Strait of Gibraltar. The entire area of the sea is nearly 1 million square miles. Although sources vary, it is approximately 2,200 miles long. The width varies from 100 miles to 1,000 miles. The deepest part is off the coast of Greece. The coastline extends for more than 28,000 miles. The water has a higher salt content than most oceans. There is little tidal activity in the Mediterranean Sea, which in the Bible is often called simply "the Sea" or "the Great Sea." Many islands are located within the Mediterranean Sea, including Cyprus, Crete, Rhodes, Sardinia, Sicily, Majorca, and Minorca. Even more countries border it: along the northern shore—Spain, France, Monaco, Italy, Slovenia, Croatia, Bosnia and Herzegovina, Montenegro, Albania, Greece, and Turkey; along the eastern shore— Lebanon, Syria, Israel, and the

Gaza Strip; along the southern shore—Egypt, Libya, Tunisia, Algeria, and Morocco; and there are the island states of Cyprus and Malta. Nineteen different species of whales and dolphins have been found in the Mediterranean Sea. It is also home for the Mediterranean monk seal, sponges, corals, and 400 species of fish. In Old Testament times the Phoenicians were the people who most often sailed the Mediterranean, even though the Israelites regarded it as their westernmost border. The Hebrew people were not

seafarers but were, as someone has punned, sea-fearers. Later the Romans used it extensively, referring to it as "Our Sea" or "Our Lake."

MESOPOTAMIA—

American English pronunciation: mess-oh-poh-TAYM-ee-ah. Mesopotamia is a Greek word that means "between the rivers." The two rivers implied in the name are the Euphrates and the Tigris. In Hebrew the area is called *'Aram-Naharayim*. But this term refers to only part of the larger area now known as Mesopotamia. Modern Iraq

Street of ancient Ur in Mesopotamia

covers much of what was ancient Mesopotamia. The area encompasses wide geographic conditions—from desert to forests to floodplains. Mesopotamia received scant rains, so farmers in the area relied heavily on irrigation when the two rivers overflowed. Mesopotamia lacked much in the way of such natural resources as stone, wood, and metallic ore, so it had to import large amounts of these important commodities. Various ethnic groups lived in Mesopotamia, including the Sumerians, Akkadians, and Amorites. It appears that writing was invented first in Mesopotamia and then soon after and independently in Egypt. Mesopotamian writing is called cuneiform, and Egyptian writing is called hieroglyphics. Both cultures regarded writing as a divine gift. The Mesopotamians kept many records—written on clay tablets. Archaeologists have found and translated business records, king lists, reports of wars, religious texts, and other "documents" from the area. Abram and Sarai emigrated from Mesopotamia to Canaan at God's command. During the Babylonian Exile their descendants returned to Mesopotamia—involuntarily.

MILCAH—*American English pronunciation: MILL-kah. Hebrew pronunciation: mill-KAH.* Milcah means "ruler" or "queen." The Bible refers to two women by that name. In this book Milcah was Lot's sister, the daughter of Haran, Abraham's brother, and Rebekah's grandmother. (Marrying relatives—endogamy—was commonly done in the ancient Near East.) She had a sister named Iscah. Milcah married Nahor, her uncle (brother of Haran). She gave birth to eight sons: Uz, Buz, Kemuel, Chesed, Hazo, Pildash, Jidlaph, and Bethuel. Bethuel was the father of Rebekah.

NAHOR—*American English pronunciation: NAY-hor. Hebrew pronunciation: nah-HOHR.* Two Old Testament men went by the name of Nahor, which meant "snore" or "snort." The Nahor in this book was a son of Terah (born after Terah was 70 years old) and the grandson of the other Nahor. He was also brother of Abram and Haran. Nahor mar-

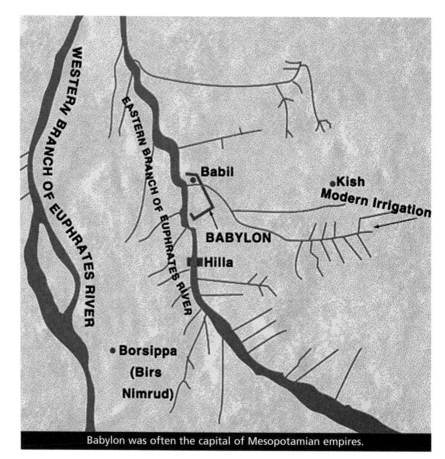

Babylon was often the capital of Mesopotamian empires.

ried his niece Milcah, who had eight sons: Uz, Buz, Kemuel, Chesed, Hazo, Pildash, Jidlaph, and Bethuel. He also had a concubine, Reumah, who gave birth to four boys: Tebah, Gaham, Tahash, and Maacah. Scholars speculate that these 12 sons became progenitors of 12 tribes just as Jacob's 12 sons became the progenitors of 12 tribes. He apparently founded the city of Nahor, which for many years scholars thought was the same as the city of Haran, but it was not.

NAHOR—*American English pronunciation: NAY-hor. Hebrew pronunciation: nah-HOHR.* In the past the city of Nahor (sometimes spelled Nahur) was thought to be identical with Haran. Now scholars recognize that they are two different locales. Tablets discovered at Mari refer to a city called *Til-Nahiri* or *Na-hu-ur* or *Na-hur* that was not far from Haran but east and south of it. It is now agreed that probably the city of Nahor was founded by Nahor himself, Abram's brother. It is here that Eliezer found a wife for Isaac.

NEGEV—*American English pronunciation: NEH-gev.*

Negev

Hebrew pronunciation: NEH-gev. The Negev (also called Negeb) is a desert (or "badlands") region that covers some 4,500 square miles. The Hebrew name means "dry." In the King James Version of the Bible, the word is usually translated as "south," because it was south of the heavily populated areas of Palestine. It was an ideal place for marauding tribes to inhabit. Kadesh-barnea is an oasis located in the Negev. Beer-sheba is its most significant city. During Abraham's time the Amalekites governed the Negev. King Solomon built

fortifications in the area. The farther south one goes into the Negev, the drier and less hospitable it gets. (Average rainfall is from two to four inches annually.) Copper is mined at Timna, the oldest copper mine in the world. Other minerals include iron, manganese, potash, phosphates, and uranium. In the highlands of the Negev archaeologists have uncovered settlements from the Early Bronze Age and the Iron Age. In the Early Bronze Age towns included as many as 200 architectural structures. In

Rachel

New Testament times the area was called Nabatea. David Ben-Gurion said that "it is in the Negev that the creativity and pioneer vigor of Israel shall be tested." When the land is irrigated, as by the National Water Carrier, which diverts water from the Lake of Galilee, the Negev becomes an excellent agricultural area. Wheat, barley, cotton, and tomatoes thrive here. The Negev makes up more than half of the modern land of Israel, even though it is sparsely inhabited. Bedouins have lived in the Negev for centuries. The

Hal-Bar Biblical Nature Reserve is located in the Negev. It is a wildlife park of 8,000 acres, where oryxes, addaxes, ibexes, gazelles, onagers, wolves, hyenas, foxes, and lynxes find refuge.

PENUEL—*American English pronunciation: PEN-yoo-el. Hebrew pronunciation: pe-noo-AIL.* Penuel is the name of a place and two men in the Old Testament. The Penuel (sometimes spelled Peniel) mentioned in this book is the place. It was here at a ford in the Jordan River that Jacob

wrestled all night with a "man" (also identified as an angel and God). After this experience, Jacob named the ford Penuel, and later a city was built here and went by the same name. The word means "face of God." Later when Gideon and his small army had routed the Midianites, the Israelites stopped here and asked for food as they continued to chase the enemy. The people at Penuel turned down the request, and Gideon returned and destroyed Penuel's watch-tower and slaughtered the inhabitants. King Jeroboam I (c. 924-903 B.C.) rebuilt Penuel, but it was destroyed by Pharaoh Shishak in 922 B.C. Not everyone agrees on its location, but many believe that the eastern part of Tulul al-Dhahab (or Tell edh-Dhahab) is the site of ancient Penuel.

RACHEL—*American English pronunciation: RAY-chel. Hebrew pronunciation: rah-HAIL.* Rachel means "ewe." She was Laban's daughter and the girl whom Jacob especially loved. Through Jacob's mother's side, Rachel was his first cousin. On his father's side, Rachel was his second cousin once removed. In order to win her hand in marriage, Jacob worked for Laban for seven years (he arrived penniless and so had no money for a bride price; additionally, Laban never gave either daughter the usual dowry a father paid.) To Jacob the time sped by because he had fallen madly in love with Rachel. Laban tricked Jacob on the wedding day, giving him Leah, Rachel's older sister, instead of Rachel herself, for whom Jacob had to work another seven years, though he got to marry Rachel at the end of that week. At first Rachel could not conceive, but finally she gave birth to Joseph and Benjamin, dying during the latter's birth. When Jacob and his extended family left Haran and Laban, Rachel stole her father's *teraphim*, or gods. Tradition refers to two sites for Rachel's tomb, one in Benjaminite territory (not far from Ephrathah) and one in Bethlehem.

REBEKAH—*American English pronunciation: re-BECK-ah. Hebrew pronunciation: riv-KAH.* Rebekah, daughter of Bethuel, lived in Paddan-aram (Haran) until Eliezer, Abraham's servant, found her and took her back to Canaan to be Isaac's wife. Her name may mean "to tie firmly" or perhaps "cattle." She was Isaac's cousin once removed. Rebekah was barren for 20 years before she gave birth to Jacob and Esau. She favored her son Jacob. When she died, she was buried in the Cave of Machpelah, which was the only real estate Abraham ever owned in the Promised Land. It appears that Jacob never saw his mother again once he left home and fled to Haran.

Rebekah

REUBEN—*American English pronunciation: ROO-ben. Hebrew pronunciation: re-oo-VAIN.* This male name most likely means "Look! A son." He was the first boy born to Jacob and Leah. Leah knew that Jacob loved Rachel more than he loved her, so when she gave birth to Reuben, Leah thought that from then on Jacob would love her, but Jacob continued to favor Rachel. When Reuben was older, he picked some mandrake roots (considered to have been an aphrodisiac) and brought them home to Leah, his mother. At that time, it was

Rachel's turn to spend a night with Jacob, so Leah gave the mandrakes to Rachel, who was barren, in turn for spending another night with Jacob. As a result, Isaachar was born to Leah. When Joseph's brothers wanted to kill him, Reuben worked to spare Joseph's life. Reuben had four sons (Hanoch, Pallu, Hezron, and Carmi). Although Reuben was Jacob's firstborn son, he ultimately lost the birthright privileges to Joseph's sons. Reuben's descendants, the Reubenites, were one of the tribes of Israel.

SARAH—*American English pronunciation: SAIR-ah. Hebrew pronunciation: sah-RAH.* Sarah was the half sister and wife of Abraham, daughter of Terah with another wife. (Endogamous marriages—marriage to close relatives—were considered desirable in the ancient Near East. Pharaohs sometimes married their own daughters. Marriage to cousins was quite common.) Her name meant "princess." She was about 10 years younger than Abraham and was barren for most of her life. She was about 65 years old when Abraham moved his household from Haran. When she was 90, she gave birth to Isaac. Sarah was legendary for her beauty—even in her old age—and two rulers wanted her in their harem. She died at Hebron (also called Kiriath-arba) when she was 127 years old. Abraham buried her in the Cave of Machpelah.

SHECHEM—*American English pronunciation: SHECK-em. Hebrew pronunciation: shee-KEM.* In the Old Testament Shechem is the name of three people and a city. The term in this book refers to a walled Canaanite city in central Palestine. It was situated about 40 miles north of Jerusalem and covered nearly six acres of land. The name itself means something like "back" or "shoulder." The city was located in the natural pass between mounts Ebal and Gerizim. It was the first city in Canaan Abram stopped at after he left Haran. The donkey was the sacred animal of the city and was offered as a sacrifice there. The god Baal-berith was worshipped here. Joseph was buried here. Archaeologists claim that they have found

Sarah

Shechem

evidence that people lived in Shechem as early as around 4500 B.C. When the Hebrew people left Egypt and began taking over the land of Canaan, Shechem fell to them early on. It was here that Joshua renewed the covenant with the people, the covenant God initiated originally at Mount Sanai. During the time of the judges, a temple to Baal-berith (Baal of the covenant) was situated in Shechem. During part of its early history, a temple fortress was constructed inside Shechem. This new building

had walls 17 feet thick! This temple existed for many years and appears to be the one mentioned in Judges 9. At the outset of the divided kingdom, Shechem served at first as Israel's capital city, which later was moved to nearby Samaria. In 750 B.C., during the time of the prophet Hosea, Shechem housed a shrine where Yahweh was worshipped. In 722 B.C. the Assyrians razed Shechem, but in 350 B.C. it was rebuilt. John Hyrcanus destroyed it permanently in 107 B.C. There is still a city by that

name. However, the site of ancient Shechem is located nearby at *Tell Balâtah*.

SIDON—*American English pronunciation: SIGH-don. Hebrew pronunciation: tsee-DOHN.* Sidon (also called Zidon and Saida), which still exists as the third-largest city in modern Lebanon, was the first prominent city of the Phoenicians. The name means "fishing" or "fishery," which is appropriate for a city located just off the shores of the Mediterranean Sea. Genesis 10:15 indicates that Noah's great-grandson Sidon was the progenitor of the original people living in this area. According to many scholars, the city may have been inhabited as far back as 4000 B.C., although it became a center of Phoenician culture in the twelfth century B.C. and reached its heyday during the Persian period, which was between 550 and 351 B.C. During that time a temple to Eshmoun, a god of healing, was constructed, and the remains, known as "Bustan esh-Sheikh," can be seen today. The two main deities of Sidon were Baal and Ashtoreth. When the Israelites entered the Promised Land, Sidon was to be part of the land granted to the tribe of Asher, but the Israelites were not strong enough to conquer the city. The Old Testament writers often use the term "Sidon" to refer to the entire land of Phoenicia. The Sidonians provided cedar logs for the temple that Solomon constructed. Ahab, king of the northern kingdom of Israel, married Jezebel, the daughter of Ethbaal, king of Sidon. The sand in the area lent itself to glassmaking, and the Sidonians learned how to make a purple dye from murex shells. The rich color of the yard goods dipped in this dye made it especially desirable for royalty. Jesus and His disciples visited Sidon, where He healed the daughter of the Syro-Phoenician woman. Paul spent a week in Sidon at the end of his third missionary journey. Today visitors to Sidon can see Murex Hill, which is formed from the discarded murex shells used to make the dye. In 351 B.C. Persian king Artaxerxes III set out to attack Sidon, which had rebelled against his rule. Knowing that it could not

Simeon

JACK PENNINGTON

successfully withstand the onslaughts of his marauding army, some citizens fled to Tyre, which was about 25 miles away, and those remaining in Sidon set the city ablaze. Some 40,000 Sidonians perished in the resulting inferno. Later the city was rebuilt, and under Roman rule it was called Nauarchis. At various times throughout its history Sidon has been ruled by Assyria, Babylon, Persia, Alexander the Great, the Seleucids of Syria, the Ptolemaic dynasty in Egypt, and Rome. Today the city of Sidon flourishes

with a population of 200,000. It has become famous for its crumbly cakes or cookies called "senioura."

SIMEON (Old Testament)— *American English pronunciation: SIM-ee-on. Hebrew pronunciation: shim-OHN.* Six men in the Bible—two in the Old Testament and four in the New Testament—had the name Simeon. The Simeon mentioned in this book was Jacob and Leah's second son. He was the progenitor of the tribe of Simeon. The root meaning of the name is a bit obscure. Some think it means "hearing [of prayer]" or "answering [of prayer]." Others surmise that it might be something like "little hyena animal." The name is also attested in extrabiblical sources. Simeon and his brother Levi wreaked vengeance upon the Shechemites after Shechem had raped their sister Dinah. Joseph as vizier of Egypt kept Simeon in prison until the brothers returned with Benjamin. Simeon had six sons. When Jacob, on his deathbed, blessed his sons, he condemned Simeon's cruelty and predicted that his descendants would be scattered throughout the Promised Land. The area that the tribe of Simeon occupied was actually within the territory allotted to Judah—mostly the Negev.

ZEBULUN—*American pronunciation: ZEB-yoo-lun. Hebrew pronunciation: ze-voo-LOON.* This proper noun probably means "exalt" or "exalted" or "elevated dwelling." Zebulun was the sixth son to be born to Jacob and Leah—after she had gone through a time of barrenness. He is the eponymous ancestor

of the tribe of Zebulun. Little is known about him personally. The territory allotted to the tribe of Zebulun was in the hill country of Galilee. He had three sons, who became the progenitors of three clans within the tribe of Zebulun. The tribe does seem to have become famous for providing military support. Nazareth, the city where Jesus spent His childhood, was in the region given to Zebulun.

ZILPAH—*American English pronunciation: ZIL-pah. Hebrew pronunciation:* *zil-PAH.* Zilpah may mean "(woman with) a short nose" or perhaps "drooping" or maybe "distillation from the mouth." She was Laban's maidservant, whom he gave to Leah as a wedding present when she married Jacob. When Leah, who already had given birth to four boys but couldn't seem to get pregnant again, wanted even more children, she gave Zilpah to Jacob as a concubine or surrogate mother. Zilpah then gave birth to Gad and Asher. We know very little more about her.

Zebulun

JACK PENNINGTON

RUTH REDDING BRAND

Ruth Redding Brand, assistant professor of English at Atlantic Union College in Massachusetts, has written the main stories in this book. Bible stories have fascinated her from the time she was a child. When the Review and Herald Publishing Association invited her to explore the Holy Land with the late Siegfried Horn, a world-renowned archaeologist and eminently knowledgeable tour guide, she eagerly accepted. That experience (along with a lot of research) gave her access to an authenticity of detail that makes the narratives in the Family Bible Story books live and breathe.

FINKLE PHOTOGRAPHY

Brand was raised on a dairy farm in Maine and grew up milking cows, haying, riding hefty workhorses, and pulling weeds in acres of corn and cucumbers. As an adult she has taught elementary school and junior high as well as college. Since earning her Master's degree in English, she has taught English at Fitchburg State College and Atlantic Union College.

She lives in Lancaster, Massachusetts, with her husband, Bob, and pampered cat, Sky. She is blessed with two adult children, Jeffrey and Heidi, and their respective spouses, Krista (Motschiedler) and Troy Clark. Brand loves to read, play word games, walk on the beach, and swim, but she'll drop any of these activities in a heartbeat to spend time with her granddaughter, little Miss Emma Mae Clark!

HEATHER GROVET

Heather Grovet lives in Alberta, Canada, with her husband, Doug. They have two daughters, Danelle and Kaitlin.

Grovet's hobbies include training and showing horses (she's been involved with horses since she was 10 years old), reading, and . . . talking! As you can tell from the Bible bedtime stories that she wrote for this book, writing is another of her hobbies. In fact, she has had many books published. Among these books are *Prince: the Persnickety Pony; Petunia the Ugly Pug; Marvelous Mark and His No-good Dog; and What's Wrong With Rusty?*

Grovet is happiest when she is outside on a

beautiful summer day, riding her horse. She's least happy when she has to do sewing and ironing or must take a long trip in the car.

She says that the one word that best describes her is *determined*. She writes, "God has put a lot of time into helping me with my patience, but I still need to improve. Also, I need to be careful not to get so busy that I forget to keep Him first."

Grovet advises young people: "God loves you even when you don't feel very lovable. Don't ever forget that."

LEONA GLIDDEN RUNNING

Even as a little girl, Leona Glidden Running found foreign languages fascinating. In high school she learned Spanish from an older student who taught her during lunchtime. In college she majored in French and minored in German, which she later taught at the high school level.

For four years Running worked for the Voice of Prophecy, a well-known religious radiobroadcast originating from California, where she typed scripts in Spanish and Portuguese. During that time her husband, Leif (Bud) Running, died. She felt as though she were in a tunnel for eight years. Then she fell seriously ill, and when she recovered Running attended seminary, where she learned biblical Greek and Hebrew. From there she began teaching seminary classes in biblical languages while she worked on a doctorate in Semitic languages at Johns Hopkins University.

For many years Running taught ancient languages at Andrews University in Michigan. Even after her retirement she taught Egyptian hieroglyphics, Assyrian/Babylonian cuneiform, and ancient Syriac for 21 more years. Today Running enjoys total retirement from the classroom. She encourages young people with these words: "Find your gift, develop it, and let God use it!"

Leona Glidden Running reviewed for accuracy the stories in the Family Bible Story series. She also prepared the pronunciation guide at the end of this book.

CONSTANCE CLARK GANE

Born in Brunswick, Maine, Connie moved with her parents (Richard and Virginia Clark) to the mission field when she was only 6 years old. She lived for nine years in Nepal, followed by two years in Pune, India.

Gane attended Pacific Union College, where in 1986 she received her bachelor's degree in music with an emphasis in violin. For the next two years she and her husband, Roy, lived in Israel, where they studied at the Hebrew University in Jerusalem.

Her University of California, at Berkeley M.A. and Ph.D. degrees are in Mesopotamian archaeology. Gane has participated in archaeological excavations at Tel Dor and Tel Dan in Israel, the ancient site of Nineveh in Iraq, and Tal Jalul in Jordan. Her area of general interest is that of the ancient Near East under the dominance of the Neo-Assyrian, Neo-Babylonian, and Achaemenid empires. Specifically she specializes in *Mischwesesn*, composite creatures, found in Late Neo-Babylonian religious art.

Gane currently is assistant professor of archaeology and Old Testament at the Seventh-day Adventist Theological Seminary at Andrews University in Berrien Springs, Michigan. She and her husband are the parents of one daughter, Sarah Elizabeth. Sarah keeps her parents in touch with reality and constantly turns their eyes and hearts to Jesus Christ.

JOEL SPECTOR

Known for his images of elegance, Joel Spector was born and raised in Havana, Cuba. He left Cuba two years after Fidel Castro took over the country, arriving in the United States in 1961 at the age of 12. After graduating from the prestigious Fashion Institute of Technology, sometimes called "the MIT for the fashion industries," Spector was hired by Fairchilds Publications, working as a staff artist doing fashion illustrations. He continued his art training at the Arts Student's League, where he studied anatomy with Robert Beverly Hale and painted under David Leffel and Nelson Shanks. After 10 years of working as a fashion illustrator, Spector decided to switch to general illustrations and soon began working for major advertising agencies, as well as for magazine and book publishers. Spector began to specialize in working in pastels and developed his distinctive style in that medium.

After living most of his life in New York City, Spector decided to move his growing family to the hills of Litchfield County in Connecticut. He and his wife, Rowena, live in New Milford with their four children: Max, Ari, Jacob, and Saskia. They also enjoy their new puppy, Reina.

In addition to working at illustration, Spector is currently a staff teacher at Western Connecticut State University. He enjoys passing along to students that which he has learned from his experience in the field of illustration.

The development of each of the pieces of artwork in this book goes through a certain process. Joel Spector went through various rough sketches as he refined his image of Esau hunting a gazelle. All of his work is submitted to an oversight committee that reviews them and makes suggestions for possible improvements.

Here we see an electronic composite of his tight sketch and the final rendering.

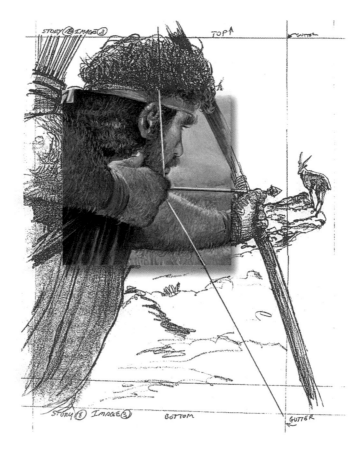

DARREL TANK

One of Darrel Tank's earliest memories of art is drawing pictures with his mother. She encouraged his creativity, which was apparent even when he was a very small child. While growing up, he often spent his afternoons at the publishing house where his father was the head photographer. The work of the illustrators there particularly fascinated him, and he began to dream of pursuing a career in art.

Tank was able to accomplish that dream in the late seventies and has exhibited and received honors at numerous art shows with his sensitive approach to portraiture. His photo-realistic style shows remarkable attention to fine detail and captures the emotion of the moment.

Tank and his wife, Denise, have four children and 12 grandchildren. They live in Garden Valley, Idaho, up in the mountains where they have snow for three to four months of the year. He writes, "We are sur-rounded by meadows, forests of pines and firs, and groves of aspens. There's a tremendous amount of wildlife, including herds of elk and deer, foxes, bears, mountain lions, wild turkeys, bald eagles, raccoons, Canada geese, and so much more."

The Tanks have an "extremely smart" yellow Labrador retriever named Chamois. She knows many tricks and loves to perform them for visitors. They also have two cats. One is 13 years old and is named Sienna, because of her color. The other is a pure white, long-haired cat.

Tank's repertoire includes black-and-white pencil renderings, color pencil, gouache, airbrush paintings, and computer illustrations, which have appeared in more than 400 books, magazines, advertising, and prints.

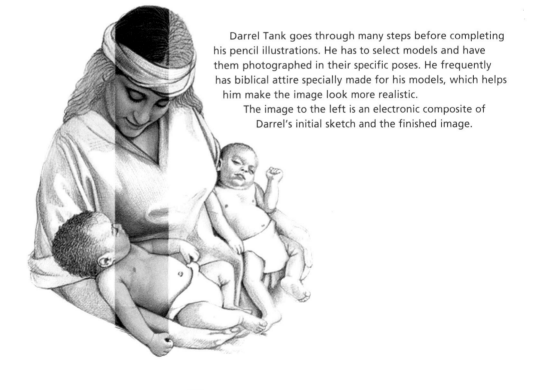

Darrel Tank goes through many steps before completing his pencil illustrations. He has to select models and have them photographed in their specific poses. He frequently has biblical attire specially made for his models, which helps him make the image look more realistic.

The image to the left is an electronic composite of Darrel's initial sketch and the finished image.

ACKNOWLEDGMENTS

Where does one begin? So many individuals have helped in the construction of this unique book. We owe all a great debt of gratitude for the time and effort they invested to make the book a reality. Perhaps we can talk in categories of influence.

RESEARCH

Gail Hunt, who had the first vision of a multilayer book and then conducted 11 focus groups around the United States

Richard W. Coffen, who brainstormed with Mr. Hunt and became director of the project

Gerald Wheeler, who as a Bible lover and book editor embraced the concept

Patricia Fritz, who spent many hours coordinating myriads of details

Bob Haddock and Associates, who helped with early marketing plans

The **many men and women and boys and girls** who shared their valuable ideas at the focus groups

ADMINISTRATION

Harold F. Otis, Jr., president who caught the vision immediately

Robert S. Smith, president who insisted on moving ahead after years of delay

Hepsiba S. Singh, treasurer who offered the financial support needed

Mark B. Thomas, vice president of the Book Division, who helped facilitate development and chaired our oversight committee

Jeannette Johnson, acquisitions editor, who kept minutes for the oversight committtee

Trent Truman, art coordinator, who prepared the layout and design and worked with the talented illustrators who provided such amazing artwork

WRITERS

Ruth Redding Brand, who researched and wrote the main stories in this series

Linda Porter Carlyle and Heather Grovet, who wrote the Bible bedtime stories

Constance Clark Gane, who prepared the time lines

Leona Glidden Running, who prepared the pronunciation guide in the glossary/Bible dictionary

Richard W. Coffen and Gerald Wheeler, who wrote the DID YOU KNOW? sections

ILLUSTRATIVE ENDEAVORS

Joel Spector   Darrel Tank

YOUNG READERS

Benjamin Baker	Nathan Blake	Annalise Harvey	Katrina Pepper	Bradley Thomas
David Baker	Coramina Cogan	Alyssa Harvey	Lisa Sayler	Jeremy Tooley
Emily Barr	Raeven Cogan	Garrick Herr	Emily Shockey	Tara Van Hyning
Jacob Barr	Rande Colburn	Alicia O'Connor	Katie Shockey	Kim Wasenmiller
Carin Bartlett	Zoë Rose Fritz	Jeremy Pepper	Jonathan Singh	Tompaul Wheeler
Caitlyn Bartlett	Jennifer Hanson	Jessica Pepper	Kaitlyn Singh	Megan Williams

SCHOLARLY INPUT

Douglas Clark	*Siegfried Horn*	*Pedrito Maynard-Reid*	*Warren Trenchard*
Larry Herr	*John R. Jones*	*Leona Glidden Running*	*S. Douglas Waterhouse*
Lawrence T. Geraty	*Sakae Kubo*	*Ronald Springett*	*Randall Younker*

LITERARY INPUT

Denise Herr, college English teacher

Kelly Bird, college student of Ms. Herr

Orval Driskel, marketer

Tracy Fry, college student of Ms. Herr

Susan Harvey, marketer

Eugene Lincoln, editor

Donna Martens, college student of Ms. Herr

Shelley Pocha, college student of Ms. Herr

Sherry Rusk, college student of Ms. Herr

Sandy Robinson, marketer

Sheri Rusk, college student of Ms. Herr

Doug Sayles, marketer

Eugene Starr, marketer

Gerald Wheeler, editor

Penny Wheeler, editor

Ray Woolsey, editor

EDITORIAL HELP

Eugene Lincoln, who helped edit and copyedit early versions

Delma Miller, copy editor

James Cavil, copy editor

Jocelyn Fay, copy editor

RESOURCE COORDINATOR

Tompaul Wheeler